CURRENT ISSUES IN ACCOUNTING AND AUDITING

Edited by

JOHN WILSON

TUDOR

This version first published in Great Britain by Tudor Business Publishing Limited.

A CIP catalogue record for this book is available from the British Library

ISBN 1 872807 07 0

Typeset by Deltatype Ltd, Birkenhead, Merseyside
Printed and bound by Biddles Ltd, Guildford, Surrey

Contents

Acknowledgements

I am grateful to my colleagues for their contributions to this text. I would also like to express particular thanks to the academics and practitioners who commented on earlier drafts of chapters and to Denise Quinn for preparing the final manuscript. Responsibility for any errors and omissions, however, is entirely mine. Finally, thanks as ever to Chris and Hannah for their patience.

John Wilson
January 1996

Notes on contributors

JOHN WILSON is Head of the Centre for Public Service Management, Liverpool Business School. He is a qualified member of the Chartered Institute of Public Finance and Accountancy (CIPFA) with an academic background in politics and economics. His main research interests concern the management and economics of public service provision, the implications of Compulsory Competitive Tendering and the impact of capital accounting in the public sector. He is author of *Public Services and the 1990s: Issues in Public Service Finance and Management* (Edited with P Hinton, Tudor 1993) and *Managing Public Services: Dealing With Dogma* (Tudor 1995). He currently acts as an academic adviser to CIPFA.

ALAN DOIG is Professor of Public Service Management and Head of the Unit for the Study of White Collar Crime, Liverpool Business School. He was previously Sub-Dean of the Faculty of Social and Environmental Studies and Fellow of Institute of Public Administration and Management, University of Liverpool. His main research interests concern corruption and fraud in the public sector, on which he has published extensively. He is the author of *Corruption and Misconduct in Contemporary British Politics* (Penguin) and *Westminster Babylon: Sex, Scandal and Money in British Politics* (Allison and Busby).

DAVID GARDNER is a Principal Lecturer, Liverpool Business School. He is a qualified member of CIPFA with an academic background in economics. His main research interests are in the areas of economic regulation and auditors' liability. He acts as an academic adviser to CIPFA and is a member of its Education and Training Executive.

BOB HOPKINS is a Senior Lecturer, Liverpool Business School. He is a qualified member of CIPFA. He has considerable practical experience at a senior level in local government. His main area of research interest is the area of audit expectations.

DR JENNIFER LEE previously lectured in business policy at Liverpool Business School. Born in Huntsville, Alabama, she was educated at Emory University where she received a BA in Economics and a BA in International Studies/French. After spending a year at the University of St Andrews as a Robert T Jones Scholar, she returned to the United States and completed a Juris Doctorate at the University of Georgia. Her main research interests are in the areas of law and economics.

DAVID NEAL is a Lecturer, University of Wales, Bangor. He previously lectured at Liverpool Business School, Liverpool John Moores University. He is a qualified member of the Institute of Chartered Accountants in England and Wales.

ROGER PEGUM is a Principal Lecturer, Liverpool Business School. He is a qualified member of the Chartered Association of Certified Accountants. He has an academic background in accounting and finance and gained considerable experience as a practising accountant in industry prior to joining higher education. He has previously taught at Manchester Metropolitan University and is a visiting lecturer to Southern Denmark Business School. His main research interests are in the area of comparative international accounting with particular emphasis on Europe.

KEN PURNELL is a Senior Lecturer, Liverpool Business School. He has an academic background in statistics and public sector economics and has considerable consultancy experience in the application and relevance of statistical techniques to public and private sector companies.

BRENDAN QUIRKE is a Senior Lecturer, Liverpool Business School. He is a qualified member of CIPFA and has an academic background in politics. He joined Liverpool Business School from the University of Keele and previously worked for the Audit Commission. His main research interest is in the area of environmental accounting.

Foreword

Accountants, auditors and the organisations within and for which they work are all currently confronted with a number of fundamental issues. The nature of the issues and the response of the accountancy profession to them need to be constructively analysed. They embrace the respective roles of the accountant and the auditor, the usefulness and reliability of the information they provide and the overlap between technical accounting matters and wider social considerations. They are also applicable, in whole or in part, to both the public and private sectors.

This text addresses a number of the main and most controversial issues. It brings together matters of direct concern to accountants, auditors and their clients. Unlike most other texts, however, which are exclusively written for either the public or private sector, this book contains analyses of topical issues which are directly or indirectly relevant to each or both sectors.

The publication will serve as an invaluable teaching text for undergraduate courses but will also prove useful for professional accountancy students.

Chapter One examines past and present attempts to construct a theoretical framework for financial reporting. The methods of theory construction will be critically evaluated and a number of alternative accounting theories will be suggested which challenge the traditional approach to financial reporting.

Chapter Two begins by placing into context the current controversy concerning auditor liability and exploring the legal responsibility of the auditor. Criminal and civil liability are then analysed, focusing on the latter. The basis of civil liability is explained and particular attention is paid to the issue of liability to third parties, demonstrating how the interpretation has developed from the Candler and Crane Christmas case in 1951 to the Caparo Industries case of 1992. More recent cases are then discussed to consider the impact of the Caparo decision on the auditing profession.

Chapter Three provides a comparison of international accounting practice, focusing on Europe. Different political, legal and economic systems are identified and their impact on accounting practice is critically analysed. Conclusions are reached as to the degree of harmonisation, mutual recognition and divergence of practice.

Chapter Four considers, on the basis of empirical research, the controversial question of audit expectations, focusing in particular on the public sector. The issue is of particular relevance given the increased competitiveness of the environment within which public service organisations now operate.

Chapter Five examines the rationale, significance and implications of the issues surrounding environmental accounting.

Chapter Six examines the ethical work environment, from audit committees to codes of conduct, which is essential to ensure probity among management and employees. It is contended that the internal audit role cannot be effectively or efficiently fulfilled unless such an environment exists. Focusing on the public sector and drawing upon case studies, the impact of change and the implications for probity are examined. The role of the internal auditor in providing organisation-wide guidance to adapt and sustain the ethical environments is critically assessed.

Chapter Seven analyses the rationale underpinning the introduction of alternative arrangements for resource accounting in the delivery of public sector services. In considering the implications of the changes and the merits of introducing commercial accounting principles, the emphasis will be placed on local government.

Chapter Eight examines the rationale of creative accounting particularly within the context of the efficient market hypothesis and positive accounting theory. Various types of creative accounting are considered and the extent to which they undermine traditional accounting is critically examined. The nature and adequacy of the response of the Accounting

Standards Board are analysed. Alternative approaches to creative accounting are also suggested.

Chapter Nine explores the continuing controversy about the role an insolvency system should fulfil in a competitive economy. The current structure of the UK insolvency system is described and areas for reform are identified. The role of the accountant in deciding upon a course of action for an insolvent business is critically evaluated.

This book is dedicated to Emma and the memory of Jock.

1

Accounting Theory

David Neal

Introduction

This chapter looks at various approaches to answering the "ancient question" (Sterling 1990) of "what ought accounting practices to be?" It does so by trying to develop, from a brief history of accounting and a review of the various attempts to construct an all embracing accounting theory, the position that accounting theory is in fact about trying to establish "preferences" (Revsine 1977). The academic area of accounting theory is a very broad one and by necessity not all the approaches that have been taken to the subject can be looked at in this chapter. Those who have grappled with the thorny question of the role of accounting have been influenced by the society in which they operate, by the current academic flavour of the month, and by ideas imported from a variety of other disciplines as well as, and perhaps crucially, by the political environment (in its broadest sense) that the accounting theorist and the accounting standard setters they seek to influence work within.

An important point to make about this subject is to define its scope and its terms. When speaking of accounting theory it is almost always the act of publicly reporting the financial performance of a limited liability company that is embodied in the term "accounting". Of course the subject area of accounting is much broader than this and in fact we are discussing "financial reporting theory". This chapter will however use both accounting and financial reporting as synonyms with appropriate apologies to those with other interests within the discipline for "hijacking" the generic term "accounting".

Historical Context

The year 1994 saw the five hundredth anniversary of the publication of Pacioli's "Summa de Arithmetica, Geometrica, Proportioni et Proportiona-lita" which reflected on the methods of bookkeeping in use by the Venetian merchants of his time. Pacioli did not, as is popularly supposed, invent double entry bookkeeping but his contribution was nevertheless vital in the "codification" and to some extent standardisation of accounting practices. He suggested that no business could be conducted successfully without a method of "systematic recording" because otherwise "they would have no rest and their minds would be troubled". Certainly it would appear that his advice was followed, for in the centuries that followed the double entry method became almost universally accepted as the method of recording business transactions.

It was not however the beauty of Pacioli's prose or his advice on avoiding stress that led to this universal acceptance; it was the logic and simplicity of the double entry method itself. Double entry is in fact a logical system of comparisons of asset with liability, of receipt with cost and so on. The inherent aim of double entry is to make these comparisons mathematically valid, where the debit and the credit are always in perfect relation. But while possessing a wonderful symmetry, looking for the answer to the "ancient question" (Sterling op cit) in the properties of bookkeeping is not helpful. In fact accounting is a very different process to bookkeeping although its roots are firmly embedded in it. Accounting is the stage before bookkeeping where a decision has to be made and preference expressed on two key decisions. The first is what to record and what not to record and the second is what weight or valuation to put on the transaction once it has been decided to record it. It is in this second area of valuation that most of the disputes arise in accounting theory.

The key concept in the valuation debate is that of capital and the changes that occur in capital. Many economists (Fisher, Hick, Lindahl et al) have struggled with the theoretical problems of defining capital, including Hick's less than prosaic coinage of the term "well-offness" to describe an individual's wealth. There are problems indeed in measuring an individual's wealth, but while the concept is important for areas of microeconomics the problem of expressing preference for one particular method of income measurement can be confined within the parameters of the utility function of that individual. The problem with accounting is that it is essentially about communicating the changes in capital (and therefore calculation of income) of an entity (be it an individual or a corporation) to others in a consistent way. Seeking consistency, clarity, relevance and reliability of the information when reporting to a diverse audience, who each have very different preferences, lies at the heart of the theory problem in accounting. Even the demands for corporate social reporting can be presented within this framework for it is the lack of recognition by current accounting practice of "social capital", and the dispute over what constitutes a businesses responsibility, that leads to the call, by some at least, for a change of outlook. The diversity and the complex requirements of the recipients of accounts also precludes any simple solution to this issue.

Pacioli himself recommended the periodic drawing up of accounts for business ventures so as to preserve friendships among the participants. Presumably any dispute over the size and definition of capitals could be resolved by mutual agreement or by recourse to the court system, because of its localised nature. The real thrust for the development of modern accounting, came with the development of modern capitalist forms of organisation and control. Weber describes this development of capitalism in the following terms.

> These two important factors are inextricably linked since the separation of ownership of capital from the day to day control of manufacturing led to a need for a monitoring system. Modern financial reporting developed to communicate the results of this monitoring.

This developed in the UK from the Joint Stock Companies Acts of 1844 and 1856 which first introduced the term "true and correct" to the accounting agenda. This legislation was basically the first piece of "investor protection" legislation which expressed a need among the owners of capital to be protected from the various scams of the early part of the industrial revolution. It was precisely because the emergent capitalists did not want to be too closely involved in the actual business of the enterprise but instead wanted the freedom to diversify and to treat their investment as a homogenous commodity in its own right that caused them to seek legislative protection both to monitor management's stewardship of capital and to ensure equality of treatment among equity investors. Financial reporting provided one of the foundations for these new social relationships and led to the incorporation of certain key, and still generally accepted, accounting principles into the accounting environment. The dominant place of conservatism and its link to current practice or income recognition can be found in this historical root.

Development of Accounting Theory

A single unitary theory of accounting does not exist but there have been a number of attempts at formulating either complete or partial theories to cover the area of financial reporting. A theory is defined by the Oxford Dictionary as a "system of ideas explaining something, especially one based on general principles independent of the . . . phenomena to be explained". There is no great and inclusive theory of the general scheme of things and most philosophers would agree that the search for a meta theory is fruitless. Instead each particular subject area will seek to develop theories to explain its own particular subject matter. It is also possible that a paradigm might in some sense be "imported" into a subject area in an attempt to interpret it. Accounting has had a distinct lack of success in developing a paradigm but has been looked at through a number of external disciplines, such as economics and sociology, from the orthodoxy of Friedman to the radical Marxist view and lately even the "postmodernism" of Foucault and Derrida.

The main attempts at forming a theory from inside the accounting paradigm have been descriptive in nature but there have been various attempts to capture the "higher ground" of a more rigorous approach to theory formulation. Sterling (Sterling 1970) adopts a "normative approach" to accounting theory to justify a set of principles that "should be" in contrast to those that "are". An alternative and antagonistic view of theory construction is that of the positive school, whose methodology was taken from a well known essay of Friedman and whose chief apologists are Watts and Zimmerman (Watts and Zimmerman 1978). This seeks to develop a theory to explain what is and precludes making statements of a normative nature because of the impossibility theorem (Demski 1973).

An alternative way of interpreting the normative/positive divide is to look at the problem in terms of a deductive/inductive approach to theory construction. The deductive approach to theory construction can be characterised in four stages.

1. Specify the objectives, "taken for granted" elements or necessary conditions for your theory.
2. Derive principles from the objectives and postulates.
3. Develop accounting standards.
4. Test the theory for consistency and empirical application.

The last of these stages is, in some ways, the most important since the theory can only be acceptable if it stands up to the demands of empirical testing. If the predictions of a theory are accurate in terms of empirical testing then it is verified; if not then it has to be rejected and the process has to be restarted. The verification of a theory is however only a temporary thing since the best level of proof is "not falsified" rather than true for all times and places. A theory can only be judged as adequate if a measurement criterion is available to establish its validity. As Sterling puts it:

> In short, theory construction and measurement development are insepara-
> ble. The theory specifies what is to be measured, how the measurements are
> to be manipulated and what measurable outcomes one can expect. This
> implies that the theory is constrained by what can be measured. (Sterling
> 1970 p456).

The inductive approach to theory construction can equally be broken down into stages.

1. Record observations of particular occurrences.
2. Analyse these observations, seeking out generic characteristics and recurring patterns.
3. Derive commonalities and principles from these characteristics.
4. Test these principles.

Again the last stage is crucial in the construction process since the testing allows the theory to claim broader support than its original narrow base of empirical data allows. So from a small sample, or one particular set of instances, we develop general principles with which we can then predict other occurrences. The validity of the theory depends on establishing the validity of those outcomes. One weakness of the inductive model is that the input of the theorist may be seen to be less than in a deductive approach since induction does not seek to cause change by theorising but to explain what is happening. In its defence it may claim therefore to be more "value free" than the deductive approach. This can be disputed by the counter claim that there is an implicit value system that is unchallenged and that mirrors the existing structure of social relations.

In the light of these tools of theory construction we can now move to examine the various attempts at constructing an accounting theory in more detail and, to some extent at least, in historical order. This is difficult since these theories are in some senses competitive and therefore concurrent in many cases. In fact the generally perceived failure to develop a "winning" theory means that many of these approaches are still competing.

GAAP

Financial reporting developed as a practical subject without an explicit theoretical framework but not without an implicit one. This implicit framework was the development of Generally Accepted Accounting Principles (GAAP) which has been the longest running and most deep seated framework within which accounting has operated. It is a descriptive theory of accounting although it might also be argued that it is "evolutionary" (Accounting Standards Board 1991a).

The Accounting Principles Board of the American Institute of Certified Public Accountants (AICPA) in its Statement No.4 states GAAP arose from "experience, reason, custom, usage, and . . . practical necessity" and that it "encompass(es) the conventions, rules and procedures necessary to define accepted accounting practice at a particular time". The emphasis in GAAP is very definitely on practice forming theory, the idea being that the preparers and auditors of financial statements will develop innovative solutions to accounting issues as they arise, which by a system of dissemination and discussion (which is undefined) will then be adopted as best practice. The process therefore could be seen as evolutionary and responsive, flexible and democratic.

The problem with GAAP is whether it can correctly be called a theory, since no definition of "best practice" can be found which is truly independent from the phenomena to be explained as the definition requires. A technique is best practice because it is GAAP and it is GAAP because it is best practice, the circularity being obvious. The other main criticism of GAAP is that it assumes some sense of neutrality (Solomans 1991) in the adoption of best practice and ignores the key question of in whose best interest the practice to be adopted will be. This is the problem of the "politicisation" (Horngren 1973) of accounting standards and in the absence of a proper theory for determining best practice from an "outside source" it is impossible to resist the pressure to meet the demands of particular interest groups on each issue. This has led to the adoption of standards which are contradictory. This is best illustrated in the UK by SSAP12 "Accounting for Depreciation" which prescribes that all assets should be amortised, followed by the introduction of SSAP19 "Accounting for Investment Properties" which states that this type of asset should not be depreciated. This is because a normative argument cannot be refuted by another normative argument as the problem of incorrigibility is hit head on.

It was the search for a frame of reference outside that of best practice that lead, and still leads, regulators throughout the world to search for a conceptual framework of accounting which would help them to resist undue pressure and have a more definite guide for informing best practice.

The Conceptual Framework Project
To separate the conceptual framework project from GAAP seems at times to be difficult because of the position adopted by the standard setting bodies involved in this project. The key players in this development have been the Financial Accounting Standards Board in the USA, followed both chrono-logically and intellectually by the Accounting Standards Board of the UK and the International Accounting Standards Committee.

One of the latest incarnations of the conceptual framework project was the publication of an Exposure Draft Statement of Principles by the UK Accounting Standards Board (ASB) (Accounting Standards Board 1991b) which specifically acknowledges its debt to the FASB and to the IASC in its preface. All of these bodies are acknowledged as coming to substantially the same conclusion which is hardly surprising given that in its own Statement of Aims the ASB (Accounting Standards Board 1991a) favours an evolutionary approach rather than a process of revolutionary change. This Statement of Principles is therefore being practised within an implicit framework where principles and practices are modified and accepted over time because of their alleged usefulness and compliance with user needs. This framework allows for constant re-evaluation, monitoring and modification in the practice of financial reporting to provide further input to the theory, leading eventually to a better and more appropriate theory.

The ultimate position would be that, by constant verification of actual outcomes of reporting practice and subsequent modification of theory, a "better" theory will emerge. The process of evolution and the ability to "verify" outcomes against undisputed criteria (derived from a series of objectives outlined by the standard setters for accounting practice) will eventually lead to a unified and accepted theory of accounting. This all-embracing conceptual framework will then be a point of reference for justifying existing accounting standards and for developing new standards with the minimum of controversy, as outlined by the ASB in its exposure draft (Accounting Standards Board 1991b paragraph 1).

The approach of "the conceptual framework project" is that of deductive theory construction. Referring back to the stages of theory construction using this method it can be shown that the first stage is the outlining of the objectives of financial reporting and in this too the ASB has largely, although somewhat belatedly, followed the FASB and IASC model.

The objectives outlined for financial statements by the ASB could be argued to be based on common sense and pragmatism, and also seek to produce a consensus on the nature of financial reporting. However this is in fact a major problem in that they also exclude alternative approaches on the grounds of normality. The Exposure Draft Statement of Principles is not an attempt to begin from scratch and examine financial reporting in any fundamental sense but is an attempt to justify existing practice. From this comes a vital criticism of the conceptual framework exercise, that it fails to start from first principles because the standard setters have been the subject of a political process aimed mainly at protecting the vested interest of the major audit firms and their client managers.

The ASB Statement of Principles

The ASB in fact have tried to distance themselves to some extent from the "conceptual framework" by instead calling their current contribution a "Statement of Principle". This is to provide a framework for the drafting of Accounting Standards and consists of seven chapters on the following subjects, none of which have yet progressed further than the draft phase.

1. The objectives of financial statements.
2. Qualitative characteristics of financial information.
3. The elements of financial statements.
4. The recognition of items in financial statements.
5. Measurement in financial statements.
6. Presentation of financial information.
7. Reporting entity.

The criticism that follows will focus on chapter two, qualitative characteristics, as the context of the other chapters is beyond the scope of this chapter. However, it should be noted that chapter five, on measurement, has been issued in draft and is the cause of much debate.

The Limitations of the ASB Statement

In the introduction to the Statement of Principles the reference to existing practice and by implication the exclusion of alternatives starts almost straight away. Financial statements are narrowly defined as "prepared and presented at least annually and are directed towards the common needs of a wide range of users". (Accounting Standards Board 1991b para 6). This implies the acceptance of producing just annual and interim statements. It then goes on to explain that "some users may require, and may have the power to obtain, information in addition to that contained in the financial statements" (Accounting Standards Board ibid para 6). Here we have a major limitation of both the scope and purpose of financial statements and an implied definition of financial statements as limited to that which already exists. What has in fact begun is a definition of financial statements without reference to the objectives which will be outlined in chapter 1 of the draft. The extent to which the objectives can be met is limited by the definition of financial statements which themselves are the "normality" that the objectives seek to reflect. The objective and the subject are completely interlinked and self-referencing.

Further limitations which can be found include a definition of users and identification of their needs, which is extremely short and vague, followed by the statement that ". . . all the information needs of these users cannot be met by the financial statements" (Accounting Standards Board ibid para 10) and continues that "there are needs common to all users" (ibid para 10). The implication of this is therefore that only common needs will be provided and this is then further qualified by "awarding primacy to investors" (ibid para10), implying that only informational needs in common with the investor group will be met. This is an example of a "Dominant Group Interpretation of Accounting Objectives" (Dopuch and Sunder 1980) and provides further evidence of the real purpose of the Statement of Objectives which is to justify existing practice. This is followed by an acknowledgement that information exists which is vital to the management that is not in the financial statements and which by implication will not be reported (Accounting Standards Board op cit para 11), reinforcing the role of these definitions as a way of excluding consideration of areas not covered by the existing framework.

Qualitative Characteristics – Problems of Definition
Having identified the aims of financial statements the draft Statement of Principles goes on to address "The Qualitative Characteristics of Accounting Information". This introduces certain key characteristics which financial reporting practices should meet but in terms that largely defy definition in any strict way. The words used as qualitative characteristics such as relevance and reliability, which are deemed to be the primary qualities of financial statements, are capable of definition only in a subjective way. The premise in the use of such terms is there is general acceptance of the meaning within the accounting context. The evidence from the standard setting

process in both the UK and the USA would seem categorically to contradict this.

Decision Usefulness

One of the underlying precepts of the conceptual framework project is that of decision usefulness, the assumption that the purpose of accounts is to provide input into some great but unspecified user decision model. The users are defined and then the output in the form of standards can be observed, but there appears to be little (rigorous) connection between the two. Some have however tried to take the decision usefulness concept and tie it into specific user needs derived from Capital Market Theory or empirical research into user requirements. Examples of this include "The Corporate Report", Arnold and Hope, *Accounting and Business Research* 1975 and the ICAS report "Making Corporate Reports Valuable" 1989. All of these reports have tried in some way to construct an ideal set of decision useful data based on the users and the objectives of the ASB Statement. The outcome is an emphasis on forecast information and on management prediction of the uncertainty in these forecasts with very little emphasis placed on any of the balance sheet values or income figures produced under current accounting principles. One interesting thing to note about these attempts to align accounting with the market valuation of share capital has been its failure to reach the agenda of the regulators. This is indicative of a type of censorship where ideas which threaten the status quo are marginalised. In the case of Arnold and Hope this negation or censorship was imposed not only from outside but also internally with an explicit acknowledgement that their proposals were too radical and therefore would not be able to be pursued. In the world of financial reporting the passive, reactive and negative concepts are everywhere dominant: "utility", "adaptation" and "regulation" serve as the major explanatory motifs (Cooper and Burrell 1988 p99).

Another explanation of why this censorship exists is that certain proposals may actually threaten the existence of the regulators themselves and the more market-driven the solution the more threatening to the position of the regulator. Tinker (1985) describes a shift from fiduciary accounting to market-driven solutions as a retrograde step and, although the members of FASB and ASB would be unlikely to call on Tinker for support given his Marxist position, on this point they are likely to agree with his conclusion and block any attempts to end regulation as we know it.

The Events Approach

The alternative way of looking at decision usefulness is to end the second-guessing and simplification of user needs and decision models and instead to acknowledge that they are too detailed and varied to determine. This is the essence of the "events approach" advocated by George Sorter in his role on the committee of the American Accounting Association which produced "A Statement of Basic Accounting Theory" (Sorter 1969). Sorter was in a minority of one for much of the work of the committee and contrasted his views with those of the "value" or "user-need" approach, which as shown above is still the dominant school of thought in accounting theory. The value approach was based on user needs being known so that we can deductively arrive at an optimum income or capital value.

The events approach would limit as far as possible (an important caveat) the assignment of weights and values by the accountant and disaggregation would be the watchword. As far as possible, users would have raw data available from which they could draw their own conclusions within their own decision models. Aggregation destroys potentially useful information, much of which is then "rediscovered" by the financial community at a high cost. That the professional analyst has more sophisticated forecast models than can be generated from standard reports seems in little doubt so at the very least an events approach might reduce the cost of obtaining the information required for an efficient market.

However, panacea it is not. There are a number of areas that would merit further research. The most basic of these is what constitutes "an event". Difficulties revolve around the degree of detail to include without completely swamping the user, the method of presentation and how far this could be standardised, and whether to include events and costs external to the enterprise. Events would still need to be classified and identified with regard to their basic dimensions or attributes. Therefore a statement of classification would be needed to show the user how information has been grouped. One useful classification would be the degree of stability surrounding an action (Johnson 1970). Sales of trading stock by a retailer could be aggregated over a reasonable time horizon as each transaction is almost identical to the previous one. Other factors such as the weather, or the sex, age and religion of the sales assistant for each sale are unlikely to be included as the cost benefit and information requirements would preclude their use. However, sales which would not be repeated, such as those of land or other productive assets, would be individually identified by item. Full details of each individual sale with no amalgamation would be required to be disclosed within the bounds of materiality.

Overall the events approach offers the benefits of a more integrated approach to accounting and would allow for new forms and methods of analysing company performance and promoting "transparency" in the actions of the corporate sector since more detailed vetting of management information would be possible. If the level of disaggregation could be correctly set then the whole community of users could become an "audit" function. What is certain is that the events approach would involve a tremendous expansion of the data in financial reports, and possibly if knowledge is power a change in the locus of power. The recipients of information would be better placed in relation to managers in whom most power now resides. The information that the draft Statement of Principles implies is privileged to management (Accounting Standards Board 1991b para 11) would become publicly available.

The events approach also supports rather than contradicts the statement at the beginning of chapter 6 of the draft Statement of Principles that it is a

> . . . . . fundamental principle indeed that knowledge is always gained by the orderly loss of information, that is condensing and abstracting and indexing the great buzzing confusion of information that comes from the world around us into a form we can appreciate and comprehend (KE Boulding 1970).

The argument put forward by the events approach is not to end classification and ordering of information, but rather to limit the loss of information of traditional accounting presentation which carries the abstracting process so far that it no longer represents the reality that it purports to. The problem with the events approach is that it requires some sort of cost/benefit model, which would be very difficult to determine without knowing the benefits to the user's which implies some understanding of the users decision model. This itself contradicts the purpose of the approach. The pointer towards less aggregation though is useful and would find favour with a number of divergent views on accounting theory.

Positive Accounting Theory and its Critics

Another significant approach to accounting theory is that of Positive Accounting Theory. The main apologists of this theory are Watts and Zimmerman (1978, 1986) and in recent years it might be said that it has become the dominant paradigm, at least in terms of published output, in mainstream journals. However it does not enjoy that dominance unopposed, with Sterling (1990) one of its main critics, along with its rejection by those with a more radical perspective (Tinker, Merino and Niemark 1982).

Positive Accounting Theory (PAT) makes its claims based on the two pillars (Sterling ibid p100) of value-free study and the study of existing practices. Both of these pillars are vehemently rejected by the critics. The basic tenet of PAT is that theories should be developed that explain the actual accounting practice in terms of the choice made by managers of accounting procedures. The thrust is to explain why choices were made and therefore why certain standards where adopted. In doing this it is assumed that the "players" in the standard setting process are utility-maximising rational micro economists, and therefore no value judgement needs to be made with respect to the choices made. From this basis other accounting theories are seen as "unscientific" because they are normative.

The claim to be value free is vehemently attacked by Sterling (1990) who claims that PAT uses an outmoded view of science and that, in fact, neither science nor economics would unreservedly support their position. The radical critique (Tinker et al 1982) is that even if PAT could claim support from existing rational scientific practice this would not in itself provide a conclusive theory of accounting since that theory would be transitory and based on the subjective view of the theorizer, being inherently a normative proposition. On the second point Sterling and Christenson (1983) attack PAT as a theory about accountants rather than a theory of accounting, developing the cartographer analogy of Solomans (Sterling ibid p101); accusing PAT of "falling in love with the picture (financial statements), without that they need (to) be images of matter (economic goods)" (Sterling ibid p101).

So what is the essential content of PAT? The main thrusts of the hypotheses put forward have been to seek those factors that most influence management behaviour. Any given standard can then be assessed in relation to its effect on these factors and the reaction of the parties involved in the standard setting process may then be predicted. Managers' choices can be explained by the nature of the agency relationship that they have with shareholders and bondholders. Auditors' choices might be expressed in terms of the possible fee impact of standards and the risk that a standard might lead to or prevent possible negligence action against the audit firm. Regulators' choices might be expressed in terms of the influence of key constituencies on the regulators and the relative power of those bodies. For example it could be predicted that the standard setters will be more heavily influenced by the big audit firms and government lobbying than by the current academic debates taking place. Some support for this could then be found in the failure of Corporate Social Reporting to advance from an academic talking point to the "real" standard setting arena. Other hypotheses could be developed and tested from these assumptions and there is no doubt that some of the empirical findings are of great interest.

In fact Watts and Zimmerman also go on to develop a Positive Theory of Accounting Standards (1979). The demand for accounting theories is said to be a demand to satisfy the requirements of special concessions to particular interest groups. This means that theory itself is an economic good and its supply is determined by market forces (in this case the political market in its broadest sense). This criticism of other accounting theory is the one that in itself has caused the most determined attack on PAT, particularly on its claim to "scientific impartiality" (Sterling 1990 and Christenson 1983, Tinker et al 1982). It would be interesting to know whether a positive theory could be developed which could explain the behaviour of Sterling et al in making this attack.

The theory put forward by Sterling (1990) as an alternative is that of the "shamelessly stolen, 'Sterling's scapel'" which is that "any accounting concept that does not have a common-sense core that you can explain to yourself should be discarded" (Sterling op cit p133). The argument could then be developed against the use of jargon in accounting. Jargon, disguised as reason, is one way in which power is exerted over those who may be less fluent in the mastery of it. However as a general appeal to "common sense" in the formulation of accounting theory it is in danger of having the same restrictive outcomes as PAT, namely an inherent conservatism and very few if any meaningful results. The reason for this is that while "commonsense" is an appeal for a normative approach it is also an appeal to an ultimate "reason" or human logic that is not specified within the theory. The person who identifies himself as "reasonable" and "sensible" is in fact the result of a specific historical and cultural context. The analysis of any theory becomes self-referential, where seemingly universal views would in fact be those of one particular group, in this case those interested in financial reporting theory, who almost certainly are drawn from a very narrow band of experience.

While accepting his criticism of PAT as valid we can then observe that Sterling falls into a classic modernist "trap" in both criticising Watts and Zimmerman for not having (or even desiring) a theory to explain choice between alternative financial reporting procedures and then proposing a methodology which then fails to meet his own criteria of being capable of being measured (Sterling 1970). Sterling in fact could be argued to be heading even further in the direction of classical economics than Watts and Zimmerman since his appeal to "commonsense" is in fact an appeal to the implicit framework of current accounting practice based upon decision usefulness criteria that are themselves founded in the desire to provide more information into an economic model that is essentially neo-classical (the dividend valuation model).

The Radical Paradigm

The radical paradigm in accounting theory is probably best represented in the work of Tinker, who among others has tried to bring a Marxist interpretation to the role of accounting. Others such as Hoskins have criticised this approach as too determined by materialism and class conflict and have attempted to apply the work of such social philosophers as Foucault to this subject area. This has in itself produced a fierce debate within the those elements of the academic accounting community that can loosely be grouped under the radical banner (see *Critical Perspectives on Accounting* vol 5 1994). Other significant work in the radical tradition has also been performed in the area of management accounting, particularly looking at accounting with regard to its controlling role concerning labour (see Loft in D. Ashton, T. Hopper and R. Scapens (ed) *Issues in Management Accounting* 1991). This chapter will however primarily deal with Tinker's criticism of current accounting and accounting theorists.

The central themes of Tinker's work establish the importance of accounting in the social scheme for adjudicating interrelationships within society and an attempt to outline an emancipatory framework for accounting practice. In doing so he seeks to go beyond the narrow technical limits of much current accounting scholarship and "debunk" accounting by exposing its social, human and moral malaise. No-one would doubt that this is both an ambitious project and a contentious one, as Tinker seeks to show that the commitment to individualism and the many attempts to justify accounting as "objective" are attempts by theorists to exempt accounting from taking a role in social disputes or "class conflict". Accounting is in fact no more than "a social artifact" (Tinker 1985 p106) which takes its shape from the contemporary struggle over the social surplus or distribution of wealth.

The key tool for this analysis is Marx's theory of unequal exchange. This is itself a development of the Labour Theory of Value used by Marx to illustrate how value is added in the productive process. In this context as capitalism developed and industrialisation enabled increased efficiency, this generated a "social surplus" above and beyond that needed to maintain basic existence. The destination of this "social surplus" then became the arena for a struggle over who should appropriate it. Marx's argument was that in capitalist society this appropriation fell to capitalists who through their ownership of property rights took the surplus which they themselves did not produce. The surplus was actually produced by labour, but labour had been reduced to a commodity through its separation from the tools or means of production. This separation from the means of production and the reduction of labour to a commodity were the principal constituents of what Marx called alienation. For Tinker accounting and accounting theory had both conspired with, and through a process of "praxis" (the intertwining of theory and practice) helped to develop, the social relationships which support the unequal exchanges of capitalism. Value theory and accounting are closely related because they determine the degree of reciprocity in an exchange both from a social and an individual point of view.

The argument is obviously more sophisticated than can be summed up in a few paragraphs but the results of Tinker's analysis is to call for a move to a more emancipated form of accounting that would be sensitive and "revealing" of the different types or levels of alienation. A side-effect of this would also be to change the direction of any research into accounting theory by acknowledging the role of accounting in this process and abandoning the search for an "objective" framework. As Tinker himself put it "Theorising is inevitably partisan – a palpable fact that has yet to register on the research agenda" (Tinker 1985 p165). The Marxist framework of alienation allows Tinker to construct a hierarchy of alienation and therefore a hierarchy of accounting systems. An accounting theory is judged by how far it contributes to the goal of an "emancipatory" accounting.

When we look at the detail of this analysis the first interesting point to note surrounds the concept of wealth misspecification, forms of alienation and accounting systems. This form of alienation arises where, because of incomplete information available to investors, the "true" economic value of the entity cannot be identified. This can be characterised in two ways, firstly in the impossibility of obtaining the ideal information set, since only perfect foresight would be sufficient to obtain such data, and secondly as failure by the market to provide the "next best set" to enable *all* investors to have an equal chance of making a well-informed estimate. The idea (supported by many case studies and much preventative legislation) is that directors and other privileged insiders are free to make exorbitant profits at the expense of other investors not so privileged. It is unfortunate that the examples used to support the case against concentrating on the development of accounting systems to combat this type of alienation involve widespread fraud of investors (Tinker 1985 ch5) since a more persuasive case might be joined by seeking to show that the whole functioning of the market depends to some extent on exploiting information advantages even if they are only marginal and that these are not available to all players. In fact the only sensible trade for speculative gains would be one where there is a perceived information advantage. Insider trading laws framed by various regulatory agencies are therefore in place merely to stop the most politically embarrassing cases rather than to stop the practice in its entirety. However the key point that flows from this is that much of the research that has been carried out in the field of current value accounting models (Edwards and Bell, Sterling, Macdonald etc.) and on the specification of improved accounting systems (Arnold and Hope, McMonnies etc.) is moving in the wrong direction! The idea that the crisis in accounting can be reduced to a merely technical issue is one that has attracted much support (Solomans and the cartographer analogy) but Tinker and others (Cooper and Scherer 1984) have argued that only a political economy of accounting would be sufficient to address the issues involved.

The second level of alienation is that of fiduciary alienation, caused by the separation of ownership from control. As we have discussed earlier this was the stimulus for the development of modern financial reporting which is meant to redress the resultant imbalance between agent and principal. However the failure of the stewardship model and the grafting of the decision usefulness concept onto the accounting "stem" from the conceptual framework project have been the major causes of the interest in developing "better" accounting systems.

The third level of alienation is that of intra-class and externalisation alienation, with the resultant accounting system being Social Constituency Accounting. This would highlight the alienation of five key groups namely capital providers, the community, customers, employees and nation states. A method of accounting to combat this involves the identification and inclusion of "externalities" into the cost structure of the firm. The aim would be to show the true effect of the company's operation by identifying costs which it imposes on others, for example the cost of both past and present pollution on the community or the true effect of unfunded pension promises on employees. However there are two key problems in this societal accounting framework, both recognised by Tinker, these being the development of a "recognition criteria" for externalities and the valuation methods to be adopted. Besides these technical problems (which are by no means trivial) there is another problem for Tinker in that this type of accounting although better than existing practice is insufficient to be truly emancipatory. This is best illustrated in his attack on Gray et al (Tinker 1992) and other advocates of what he calls "the middle ground" on corporate social reporting.

The fourth and highest form of alienation is capitalist alienation and the highest form of accounting is therefore one which would include the information necessary to recognise the alienating effects of a capitalist economic structure and would therefore, as the name implied, be a catalyst for the end of that same structure. The principle form of alienation at this level is that of the expropriation of surplus value by capital and the inefficiency and social "costs" that result from the division of labour within the capitalist economy. Tinker also believes that the problems of externalities are overcome at this level since they can be objectively based on existing social conditions that include a more egalitarian social order.

In summarising the work of Tinker it is not surprising that a similar conclusion is reached to that which has been reached by many scholars on Marx, that as a critique of the existing system it has a great deal to say and provides many useful insights. In particular it highlights a failure of the financial reporting profession to take full account of the public good element of accounting and to critically question the underlying assumptions on which many accounting ideas are based. The great weakness however is that its alternative model is only briefly described in terms of capturing the "truth" of surplus value and aiding the emancipatory process. Little detail is given of the type of output or the preferred accounting system and little is made of the problems to be encountered in putting it into practice. The idea that externalities can be objectively determined is not supported in any way by analysis of the process by which this could be achieved. The analysis produced by others in the radical paradigm based on Foucault and the power/knowledge relationship also fall into the trap of providing good critical analysis while providing little in the way of alternatives, although in their case they may fall into this trap more willingly (Niemark 1990).

Conclusion

In this brief overview of the area of accounting theory we have looked at a diverse range of approaches to the construction of an accounting theory and it would seem that it may be difficult to draw any general conclusions. There is however one common strand that links all these various theories and that is that they are all disputed. In fact as we stated at the beginning the various attempts at constructing an accounting theory are in fact an attempt by the theoriser to establish his preferences as those which should be adopted by the general audience for accounting. Revsine looks at this "preferability dilemma" (Revsine 1977) and states that as any objectives are based on beliefs and values (are normative) then there can be no single theory of accounting. Accounting is not "out there" waiting to be discovered in the way that sub-atomic particles might have been, but is a social construct. The way in which theorists approach accounting is therefore dependent on the preconceptions which they bring with them or on the paradigm which they choose to adopt. Where this is obvious as in the radical paradigm then it is easier to be clear on the objectives of the theory, but the claim by Positive Accounting Theory to be value free must be, and has been, scrutinised and found lacking. Belkaoui has described accounting as a "multi paradigm science" and while the use of the term "science" may be misleading and disputed, the description "multi" would seem to be most appropriate, and is likely to remain so.

References

Accounting Standards Board (1991 a) Exposure Draft "Forward to Accounting Standards" *Accountancy* September, pp 104–105

Accounting Standards Board (1991 b) Exposure Draft – Statement of Principles "The Objective of Financial Statements and the Qualitative Characteristics of Financial Information" *Accountancy* September, pp 99–103

Arnold, J. and Hope, A. (1975) "Reporting Business Performance"*Accounting and Business Research* Spring, pp 96–105

Belkaoui, A.R. (1992) *Accounting Theory* Third Edition, London, Academic Press

Benbasat, I. and Dexter, A.S. (1979) "Value and Events Approaches to Accounting : An Experimental Evaluation" *The Accounting Review* October, pp 735–747

Benston, G.J. (1982) "Accounting and Corporate Accountability" *Accounting, Organisations and Society* 7, pp 87–105

Christensen, C. (1983) "The Methodology of Positive Accounting" *The Accounting Review* January, pp 1–22

Cooper, D.J. and Sherer, M.J. (1984) "The Value of Corporate Accounting Reports: Arguments for a Political Economy of Accounting" *Accounting Organisations and Society* September, pp 207–32

Demski, J.S. (1973) "The General Impossibility of Normative Accounting Standards" *The Accounting Review* October, pp 718–723

Dopuch, N. and Sunder, S. (1980) "FASB's Statements on Objectives and Elements of Financial Accounting : A Review" *The Accounting Review* January, pp 1–19

Dunn, J. (1990) "A Framework for a Framework" *Accountancy*, February

Financial Reporting Council (1992) *Second Annual Review – The State of Financial Reporting* London, Financial Reporting Council

Gray, R. Owen, D. and Maunders, K. (1987) *Corporate Social Reporting*, Englewood Cliffs, NJ: Prentice Hall

Horngren, C.T. (1972) "Accounting Principles; Private or Public Sector" *Journal of Accountancy* May, pp 37–41

Johnson, O. (1970) "Towards an Events Theory of Accounting" *The Accounting Review* October pp 641–653

Jones, M. (1989) "Stimulation or Revolution" *Accountancy* April pp 106–108

Lowe, E.L. Puxty, A.G. and Laughlin, R.C. (1983) "Simple theory for complex process: Accounting policy and the market in myopia" *Journal of Accounting and Public Policy* pp 19–42

McMonnies, P. (ed), (1988) *Making corporate reports more valuable* Edinburgh and London, ICAS and Kogan Page

Miller, P.B.W. (1985) "The Conceptual Framework: Myths and Realities" *Journal of Accountancy* March, pp 62–71

Pacter, P. (1983) "The Conceptual Framework : Make No Mystique About It" *Journal of Accountancy* July pp 76–88

Rutherford, B. (1990) "Measuring up to the Matchmakers" *Accountancy* February

Solomans, D. (1978) "The politicisation of accounting" *Journal of Accountancy* November, pp 65–72

Solomans, D. (1989) *Guidelines for financial reporting standards* London, ICAEW

Solomans, D. (1991) "Accounting and Social Change : A Neutralist View" *Accounting, Organisations and Society*, vol 16, no.3, pp 287–295

Sorter, G.H. (1969) "An Events Approach to Basic Accounting Theory" *The Accounting Review* January pp 12–19

Sterling, R.R. (1970) "On Theory Construction and Verification" *Accounting Review* July, pp 444–457

Sterling, R.R. (1990) "Positive Accounting: An Assessment" *Abacus* vol. 26, no.2, pp 97–135

Tinker, A.M. Merino, B.D. and Neimark, M.D. (1982) "The normative origins of positive accounting theories: Ideology and accounting thought" *Accounting, Organisations and Society* vol. 7, no.2, pp 167–200

Tinker, A.M. (1985) *Paper Prophets: A Social Critique of Accounting* London, Holt, Rinehart, Winston

Tweedie, D. (1983) Review of "A Conceptual Framework for Financial Accounting and Reporting" *Accounting and Business Research*, Summer, pp 238–239

Watts, R. and Zimmerman, J. (1978) "Towards a positive theory of the determination of accounting standards" *Accounting Review* January, pp 112–134

Watts, R. and Zimmerman, J. (1979) "The demand and supply of accounting theories: a market for excuses" *The Accounting Review* February pp 273–305

Woolf, E. (1990) "That Elusive Conceptual Framework" *Accountancy* February, pp 63–64

2

Auditor Liability

David Gardner

Introduction

In 1993 in the United States, claims against auditors of up to $400m were settled against one of the big six UK accounting firms, with further claims in the pipeline exceeding $600m (*The Economist* 26 February 1994). Minet, the insurance broker, estimates that the proportion of litigation costs to audit fees for the "big six" has risen steadily from 2.6% in 1983 to 8% in 1993 and higher in 1994 (although according to Mitchell et al 1994 these proportions cannot be verified as the firms do not publish audited information). Not surprisingly, the large accounting/audit firms have become extremely concerned with the escalation in litigation costs in the US, Europe and Australia. There is a real chance that firms will collapse according to Ian Brindle, a Senior Partner of Price Waterhouse and former chairman of the Accounting Practices Board. "The Big Six could become the Big Three within a very short space of time" (Jack 1994a). His firm's involvement with the BCCI scandal with its huge losses may have served to heighten his concern.

The difficulty appears to have arisen because the laws of most OECD and European Union countries permit "aggrieved investors to sue a raft of parties" who may have had something to do with a company going under (*The Economist* 26 February 1994 p103), owing to their "Joint and Several Liability." Directors of such companies have limited liability, whereas only the auditor is required by law to take out the maximum insurance cover available. He or she is the party with the "deepest pockets" and is obliged to incur the greatest liability.

It is vital for the reader to understand the nature of this legal liability and how legal developments have modified it in recent years. Only then can a discussion follow on how the profession can respond and is responding to this threat. This chapter outlines the types of liability faced by the auditor, namely criminal and the much more threatening civil liability, and the principle of reasonable skill and care, before discussing at length the developing controversy over liability to third parties.

Criminal Liability

Very few of the large recent claims and settlements have involved criminal liability. In the UK, there are three sets of circumstances where an auditor might be criminally liable. First, he may be guilty of an offence under the Theft Act 1968 if he knowingly aided or abetted the management of a client firm in publishing false statements with the intent of defrauding shareholders or lenders. Second, he might be guilty under the Companies Act 1985 if he is a party to the carrying on of a business with the intent to defraud. Third, he might be guilty under the Financial Services Act 1986 if he associates knowingly or recklessly with an inaccurate or misleading invitation to invest in a client company.

Unless the auditor deliberately abuses his position by involving himself in a fraudulent scheme, he is unlikely to be guilty of a criminal offence and incur criminal liability for which he might be fined or imprisoned and expelled from his professional body.

What is Reasonable Skill and Care?

Most litigation involving auditors does not involve deliberate action. Rather it involves accusations of negligence under long established common law principles in that the auditor may have failed to apply "reasonable skill and care" in the conduct of his work, "a rather nebulous but vital quality" (Woolf 1994 p12), but the best currently available for judging the effectiveness of the auditor's work. For this he might face professional disgrace but also the much more expensive risk of civil liability, though few cases are resolved publicly through the courts, most audit firms preferring to settle out of court to avoid damaging publicity.

The basis of this is alluded to in the Companies Act 1985 which refers to the auditor's "opinion" on the truth and fairness of financial statements and the adequacy of a company's accounting records. He is not required to provide a guarantee. This is because of the need for the auditor to exercise discretion in the amount of checking and testing needed to support his opinion in the light of time, cost and evidence availability, and also because of the general subjectivity of accounting. However, he must carry out his work so effectively that he stands a "reasonable chance of discovering a material error in the figures" (Dunn 1991 p40). This is the essence of the requirement for "reasonable skill and care" to be shown by the auditor.

The difficulty arises in demonstrating what constitutes reasonable skill and care. Precedent is limited by the high proportion of cases settled out of court, and by the fact that ongoing developments in accounting, auditing techniques and business practice have meant that older precedents may no longer apply and that higher standards are continually being expected of auditors. However, the fundamental need to apply reasonable skill and care remains unchanged. The *Kingston Cotton Mill* (No2) 1896 case established this principle but, whilst in 1896 an auditor might not be deemed to be negligent, despite not attending a major stock count and missing a large error, today a similar omission would not be sanctioned. The Auditing Guideline of 1983 (Auditing Practices Committee [APC] 1983) specifies the need for an auditor to attend stock checks when stock values are material.

Similarly the judge in *Re Thomas Gerrard and Son Ltd* 1968 said "The real ground on which *Re Kingston Cotton Mill Co* (No2)(1896) is, I think, capable of being distinguished is that standards of reasonable care and skill are, upon expert evidence, more exacting today than those which prevailed in 1896" (Dunn 1991 p41). Nevertheless Lord Justice Woolf's observation in the 1896 case that "the auditor is a watchdog and not a bloodhound" makes the point clearly that the auditor must be able to demonstrate the application of a reasonable degree of skill and care.

Auditing Standards and Guidelines are published by the Auditing Practices Board (APB, formerly Committee) of the profession and whilst they are not legally enforceable (guidelines are not even mandatory), they are widely accepted as the definitive statements of what constitutes best auditing practice. As a general observation, proven compliance with Auditing Standards and Guidelines is likely to satisfy a court in demonstrating that the auditor has worked to currently acceptable standards and shown reasonable skill and care, though it does not provide an absolute defence. It is possible that a court could demand more than professional requirements. This has already happened in the USA (Gwilliam 1985) showing that subjective judgement is still required in applying professional standards. Bartlett (1994) discusses circumstances where US courts expect more than compliance with standards in order that "fairness" be demonstrated, and even where compliance itself might produce misleading statements.

Furthermore, standards may not wholly keep pace with rapid and recent technical developments as in computerised accounting systems, statistical sampling or risk-based auditing, to the extent that court decisions may inevitably require more than professional standards. These in turn may well ultimately catch up with developments in the near future (Dunn 1991).

Civil Liability

Establishing an auditor's negligence and failure to exercise due skill and care is not on its own sufficient to enable damages to be recovered from him. It is additionally necessary to demonstrate that the auditor *owed* a duty of care to the plaintiff and that the plaintiff *suffered a loss as a result* of that negligence.

Where the plaintiff is a shareholder of the auditor's client company, the existence of a duty of care is clear through a contractual relationship in which the company pays the auditor who provides assurance and reports to its shareholders. In the case of *Re Thomas Gerrard and Son Ltd* (1967), the liquidator, acting for shareholders, brought a successful action against the company's auditors for failing to spot manipulated stock balances despite suspicious circumstances involving altered records (Pratt 1982). Damages awarded reflected the resulting loss. Case law of this kind is however scarce.

It would appear that the auditor's duty of care may extend beyond shareholders to lenders, investors and many other interested parties. This is because company accounts filed with the Registrar of Companies are a public record. There are very many potential users, most of whom are not known directly by the auditor, who may, to some extent, suffer loss through an auditor's negligence. It is this area of liability to third parties that has involved increasing controversy in recent years and caused huge concern to the profession, borne out by the view of William Kinney, chair of the graduate school of business, University of Texas: "It is fair to say that litigation threatens the continued existence of independent auditing as we know it today" (Jack 1994c).

Third Party Liability

In *Candler v Crane Christmas* (1951), Candler lost his investment, following liquidation, in a company for whom Crane Christmas had prepared financial statements for the purpose of negotiating the investment. Crane Christmas had failed to verify the ownership of some buildings that were not actually owned by the company but were shown as the company's assets. They knew of the plaintiff and his likely reliance on the statements, yet the court held that the auditor had not owed a duty of care. However, a dissenting judge, Lord Denning, expressed strong disquiet over this decision, arguing that liability should extend to anyone whose use of the accounts was known to the auditor. Nevertheless, this principle survived until 1964 when Denning's view prevailed and began the procession of escalating claims by third parties.

In *Hedley Byrne and Co Ltd v Heller and Partners Ltd* (1964), Hedley Byrne requested a bank reference from Heller for a company for which Heller was banker, and with which Hedley Byrne planned to do business and needed to confirm its financial status. The reference provided contained an error and Hedley Byrne incurred a loss as a result. Heller argued that they owed no duty of care because Hedley Byrne had not paid for the certificate and were not their clients. The court decided that a duty of care was owed because Heller knew of the use to which the reference was to be put. However, they escaped paying damages because their reference contained a disclaimer of liability.

Whilst this case did not involve auditors, it established ground rules affecting all professional practitioners, including auditors, who issue reports to clients for use by others. A duty of care was now owed to a third party if the auditor was aware of the third party's interest and the use to which the audited accounts would be put.

The Institute of Chartered Accountants of England and Wales (ICAEW) promptly sought advice from Counsel as to the case's applicability. The Opinion received indicated that there was a duty of care by the auditor and hence a liability to a third party, but only if:

> it is clear that any financial loss is attributable exclusively to reliance on a negligently prepared document; the party issuing the document knew the purpose for which it was being prepared and knew, or ought to have known that it was to be relied on in that particular context.

With regard to reliance on the Audit Report, the Opinion was that, since accounts were produced for stewardship purposes only and addressed with the Audit Report to the current shareholders only, the liability did not extend to the current or potential shareholders in the context of a decision to make further investments.

> Where an accountant specifically restricts the scope of his report or expresses appropriate reservations in a note attached to and referred to in the financial statements he has prepared or the report which he has made to them, this can constitute a *disclaimer* which will be effective against any action for negligence brought against him by third parties (ICAEW 1965).

The ICAEW statement containing the above emphasised that the extent to which the accountant accepts responsibility should be made clear beyond the possibility of misunderstanding (with use being made of specific exclusions where necessary). It also stressed the need for Professional Indemnity Insurance for auditors.

Subsequent cases sought to clarify the applicability of the principles established in a non-audit case to audit circumstances and extended the auditor's duty of care further as the size of damages claims traced an upward spiral. In *Jeb Fasteners Ltd v Marks Bloom and Co* (1981), Jeb had taken over BG Fasteners Ltd whose profits had been overstated in their financial statements. This overstatement had not been identified in the audit. As a consequence, Jeb had paid an excessive price for the company. The court held that it should have been clear that BG would seek financial support, using its financial statements, as it was experiencing liquidity difficulties. The auditors should therefore have foreseen a likely takeover and the likely use of the audited accounts in fixing a purchase price. Hence Marks Bloom, the auditors, were found to have a general duty of care in spite of being unaware of Jeb's specific interest in BG (Savage 1981).

The case of *Twomax Ltd v Dickson McFarlane and Robinson* (1982) demonstrated that the duty of care of an auditor applied only where the use of audited financial statements was reasonably foreseeable (Keenan 1983). Twomax bought shares in Kintyre Knitware Ltd on the strength of recent audited accounts which contained several errors. Dickson et al, the auditors, were aware that the company needed capital and that a director wanted to sell his shares, and so had a duty of care. They were obliged to pay damages to Twomax for the loss on their investment.

This apparent crystallisation of the auditor's liability to third parties was altered significantly by the case of *Caparo Industries PLC v Dickman and others* (1990) at a time when pressure was being brought to bear by the profession in the UK, the USA, Canada and Australia for governments to take steps to restrict the scale of liability that auditors faced. In the Caparo case, an apparent limitation on that liability was established by the judgement. Caparo held a small number of shares in Fidelity PLC (S. and R. Dickman were directors of Fidelity). In 1984, it started to buy up a sizeable holding. After it started to extend its holding, Fidelity published its annual report which Caparo later argued had been produced and audited negligently. Caparo argued that the auditors, Touche Ross, owed them a duty of care as they were existing shareholders and as they should have known that Fidelity were open to takeover and that they were a potential bidder. Negligence was not contested. The court rejected the case in 1987 on grounds that no duty of care was owed. The court stated that a duty could only have existed if there was a foreseeable economic loss arising through lack of care and a close and direct relationship between defendant and plaintiff. Caparo would have had to be known to the auditor, or belong to a "limited class of persons" likely to rely on the statement. The imposition of liability would have to be fair and just in the circumstances. In this case, there was held to be no close relationship as Fidelity was a PLC and shares in it were continually traded. The auditor's duty was to the existing shareholders as a class, not as individuals.

Caparo appealed and the court reversed the decision stating that a duty was owed to Caparo as an *existing* shareholder. The auditors appealed to the House of Lords which ruled in 1990 that there was no duty of care. For a duty to exist, according to the judge, Lord Bridge, the defendant would need to be fully aware of the nature of the transaction the plaintiff had in mind; he must know that his advice or information would be directly or indirectly communicated to the plaintiff; and he must know that the plaintiff was likely to rely on the advice or information in deciding on the transaction that he had in mind (Woolf 1994 p463).

In this case, the auditor could anticipate that the plaintiff would rely on the advice or information, and was entitled to do so, subject to any disclaimer. This could however subject the auditor to a liability which would "confer on the world at large a quite unwarranted entitlement to appropriate for their own purposes the benefit of the expert knowledge or professional expertise attributed to the maker of the statement" (Weekly Law Reports 1990).

Lord Bridge observed that the auditor's report is addressed to members who could rely on it in reviewing the directors' stewardship. However, the duty the auditor owes is to shareholders as a class, not as individuals. A claim against the auditor for loss would need to be made in the Company's name. The purchase of extra shares would be an independent transaction with no connection with an existing holding. Lord Oliver concurred that the law which imposed the requirement for audit was not intended to protect the public at large (Dunn 1991 p55). It is interesting to note that Touche Ross, the auditors in the case, made an out of court settlement with Caparo of £1.35m in July 1994 to head off further legal action. They deny any negligence, a position they have maintained throughout the case (Jack 1994d).

The position was clarified further by two other cases around the time of the Caparo case. In *Lloyd Cheyham v Littlejohn* (1985) the auditor was able to disprove negligence by presenting working papers which showed that he had thoroughly and rationally dealt with the issue in question in accordance with an Accounting Standard which in the particular circumstances of this case was enough to satisfy the court. The court held that a third party should not place unreasonable reliance on the auditor's opinion. In this case the plaintiff could and should have commissioned his own investigation into the company he wished to buy.

In *Al Saudi Bank and others v Clark Pixley and another* (1990) the Caparo principles were applied and, because the auditor had not directly sent a copy of the audited statements to a bank about to grant a loan to his client, and had not been aware that the statements had been distributed, the relationship to the client was not deemed to be sufficiently close. The fact that a potential lender could forseeably come to possess statements was not enough to create the necessary relationship (Keenan 1989).

Subsequent to the Caparo case, three others have endorsed its doctrine. They are *James McNaughton Paper Group Ltd v Hicks Anderson and Co* (1991), where a duty of care was denied again because it applied to shareholders as a class not as individuals; *Berg Sons and Co and others v Adams and others* (1992), which showed that the auditor's work had been performed only to satisfy the statutory audit requirement and no more, and could not support a duty of care to a finance house that had discounted Berg's bills (O'Sullivan 1993, Penn 1991 and Woolf 1994); and *Galoo and others v Bright Grahame and Murray* (1993) which would not extend the classes of persons to whom the accountant might be liable and which reinforced the view that it must be proved that an auditor's negligence must be the "effective and dominant cause" of loss for a liability to exist (Wise 1994).

Only one case, *Morgan Crucible Co PLC v Hill Samuel and Co Ltd* (1991) has threatened to dilute the effects of the Caparo decision. The case involved a company taking over another, relying on information provided by the auditor of the target company, as in Caparo. However, in this case, the directors of the target company circularised all their shareholders forecasting a sizeable increase in pre-tax profits, supported by a letter from the auditors. Significantly, the auditors' opinion was issued after the takeover had commenced, and so the plaintiff was not relying solely on the accounts but also on these further representations. The auditor had a duty of care in that, whereas in the Caparo case the audited accounts had been drafted for one purpose but had been relied upon for a different purpose, in this case, the opinion had been relied upon for the purpose for which it was issued. The degree of proximity was such that the defendant could well be liable. The case was settled out of court (Arnheim 1991, Penn 1991).

Clearly these recent cases leave the principles established in the Caparo judgement unscathed.

The Current Controversy Over Third Party Liability

Whereas the threat to audit firms in the UK, and countries whose courts may follow English legal precedent, notably Canada (Paskell Mede 1990), appears to have receded somewhat, the huge claims made in the USA where UK based audit firms have substantial business have sharpened the case for steps to be taken to curb the liability of the auditor on grounds of fairness or equity, and of the likely damage to the necessary practice of audit if the escalation is allowed to continue.

It seems strange that auditors are almost exclusively blamed for events which are the consequence of deficiencies in company management, and for corporate loss. Pound and Courtis (1980) show that very little attention is given to audit reports in general, yet, when losses are incurred after an investment, blame is heaped on the auditor as a consequence of reliance on his report. This appears to occur because the large accounting firms try to protect themselves with Professional Indemnity Insurance, so that when a company fails, given that directors have limited liability, the auditors may well be the only ones with sufficient means to pay damages – the so-called "deep pockets" principle (Jack 1994a). Even if an auditor is found to be 1% responsible for a company's failure he may be held liable for 100% of the resulting loss if others can avoid paying their share, hardly an equitable distribution of liability.

Concern over this in the UK led to the Secretary of State for Trade and Industry in 1988 setting up a study team to examine the extent of the auditor's exposure to damages claims (Likierman 1989). The Likierman Report found that levels of claims were rising, adding to the cost of Professional Indemnity Insurance. This was having the effect of making the big firms conduct more exhaustive audits and making them more selective about who they take on as clients. Likierman made a number of recommendations which have fuelled the arguments for change.

a) Currently, an auditor can be required to bear all the losses of a plaintiff, despite the fact that others, directors in particular, were responsible in part. The law covering joint and several liability should be changed to share the loss more fairly.
b) If directors were insured, the auditor would no longer necessarily have the "deepest pockets" and attract all the blame. Companies should be

permitted to pay for insurance cover for the liabilities of their officers
and directors.

c) The law of contributory negligence should be made more clear to
demonstrate whether the contributory negligence of the plaintiff can
be used to reduce the defendant's liability in a breach of contract case.

d) The Companies Act 1985 (S310) should be modified to enable the
auditor to agree with his client a contractual limit on his liability.

The outcomes of this report were that the Companies Act 1989 amended
the 1985 Act to allow companies to insure directors and officers and that the
Law Commission is looking into contributory negligence. However, it is
currently unlikely that action will be taken to change joint and several
liability, a step opposed by the Lord Chancellor, and there appears to be
little enthusiasm for negotiated contractual liability limits. The reasons are
that such changes would make it harder for an injured party to get
compensation and that damages would be unrelated to the size of any loss.

Two developments have been taking place since 1990–91 which work in
opposite directions. First, the Caparo decision, by suggesting that auditors
might not have a duty of care to individual shareholders, has led to a debate
on whether an auditor's statutory duty and liability towards shareholders
should be widened. The European Union's Draft Fifth Directive (1990)
proposes that an auditor, having committed a wrongful act, should
compensate the shareholder or third party who suffers resultant loss. This is
explained in a Consultation Paper produced by the Department of Trade
and Industry in 1990, though it is unlikely to be acted upon. O'Sullivan
(1993) develops the argument, questioning the ability of shareholders as a
group to monitor management, even with reliable financial statements, and,
in the absence of liability to individuals, whether there is sufficient incentive
for auditors to maintain audit quality. "There appears to be some
divergence between the economic need for accurate and reliable corporate
information and the courts' reluctance to impose an onerous degree of
liability on the auditor" (O'Sullivan, 1993 p414). He expresses concern over
the possible reduction in audit quality, concern supported by the report of
the DTI Joint Monitoring Unit in February 1994 which found that 75% of
firms inspected had exhibited deficiencies in audit quality (Welsh 1994a).
He proposes *extending* the auditor's liability. The direction of extension
discussed is to third party users of audited documents, though he argues that
such a move might be counterproductive in that doing so may compromise
the auditor's ability to perform an effective and independent audit; the
auditor may become the insurer of audit users' business risks; and the

resulting uncertainty may impair the auditor's ability to purchase insurance protection. Nevertheless, a vocal school of thought exists which favours extending audit liability.

This debate has taken place alongside increasing concern over the opening up of the so-called "expectations gap" whereby auditors' views on what constitutes the satisfactory delivery and extent of audit work fall short of what surveys (eg Humphrey, Mozier and Turley 1993) reveal the public expects from an audit. Luscombe (1993 p3) suggests that "there is evidence that 'it' may be progressing into a loss of public confidence". Measures such as those proposed which may vary the depth of audit work to match the extent of liability or the size of insurance premiums need to be viewed with great caution in appreciating their effect on the public perception of audit and the quality of service that the client receives. It may be that extending liability has a detrimental effect. Further research is needed. The APB has initiated a fundamental review of the long-term purposes of auditing. Hoskins (1993) argues that measures to extend the scope of audit are only part of the answer; influencing the expectations of client companies may be every bit as important. The report on "The Financial Aspects of Corporate Governance" (*The Cadbury Report* 1992) may assist in this regard by improving communications between client and auditor if audit committees are established with non-executive directors. However, these measures alone will not help without the education of all participants in the role of audit.

The second and more purposeful development is a campaign, imported from the US and Australia, organised by the senior partners of the eight largest UK-based accounting firms, calling for government to establish a limitation on their liability (*Financial Times* 23 May 1994). The ICAEW in February 1994 took up this cause, on the firms' behalf, with the DTI, arguing for an end to the auditor's exposure to unlimited liability, and an abolition of laws (such as S310 Companies Act 1985) banning auditors from agreeing liability caps with client companies (Baker 1994a), thereby implementing Likierman's fourth recommendation. It based its case initially not just on the vested interest of the profession, but on the wider public interest, in that the collapse of a major firm under the weight of litigation would have serious consequences for confidence in the audit and accountancy profession, for the other big firms and perhaps for businesses which as a result would be unable to get their accounts audited, a view challenged by Mitchell et al (1994). It also points to the harmful reduction of choice of audit firm for client companies, an argument conveniently overlooked when Price Waterhouse and Arthur Andersen sought to merge in 1993! (*Accountancy Age*

10 March 1994). The ICAEW recognises that changing joint and several liability law would be a major undertaking and would single auditors out among the professions for favourable protection, but it argues that allowing negotiated contractual limits on liability would go some way towards reducing the problem.

There are however a number of significant arguments against allowing a limitation of an audit firm's liability. First, the ICAEW stress that other professions are not prevented from agreeing, in contract, a cap on liability. The example of solicitors is often quoted, though they have never attempted to limit their liability because they consider that they could still be found negligent and be sued, making any agreed limits irrelevant. Second, removing S310 of the 1985 Companies Act would take away a strong incentive for firms to maintain high standards of audit rigour and quality by removing the threat to partners' assets. Third, accountants have a government guaranteed monopoly of auditing (Mitchell et al 1994) designed to provide shareholders with reassurance whilst putting firms into a favourable position to charge very high fees and to market additional specialist services. They nevertheless appear to be very reluctant to go to court, where the extent of their work might be subject to detailed scrutiny when sued for negligence, preferring out of court settlements. This monopoly is implicitly provided in return for the public safeguard of S310 (*Financial Times* 23 May 1994). According to Lee (1992 p102):

> The Big Six appear to be operating within a form of audit oligopoly in which the market and price for audit services are controlled by their presence. They need to address the question of whether they want to be professionals or commercial profit-making organisations. They ignore the very real presence of an audit crisis involving huge corporate failures and fraud.

In any case, recent court decisions (Caparo et seq) have clearly viewed the auditors' situation with some sympathy.

Smaller and medium sized audit firms, however, argued against the "public interest" case on grounds that the market would rapidly adjust to the loss of a large audit firm, so that the public interest would not be threatened (Mitchell et al 1994). Others went further and criticised the motives of the largest firms in seeking protection, arguing that giving protection against being negligent removes a performance incentive for auditors (Jack 1994b) and would be anti-competitive, enabling the big firms to protect their market shares more effectively. It is suggested that some smaller firms might retaliate by trying to win contracts by levying low fees sustained by lower quality work, a practice known as "lowballing". Ultimately, the ICAEW voted to present its case to the DTI without the "public interest" argument (Baker 1994b).

The Chartered Association of Certified Accountants (ACCA) however, representing many smaller audit firms, argued in its submission to the DTI that auditors should not be protected from the consequences of their negligence. Doing so would be against the public interest. It argued that capping liability would remove an incentive to maintain audit quality. "It is better, in order to protect the quality of audit work, to allow the commercial pressures of competition to be counterbalanced by the threat of liability, should audit work be found to be negligent." (ACCA Statement to the DTI, reported in Hutton 1994). "The threat of litigation must help concentrate the mind when it comes to making sure that the audited accounts show a true and fair view as the law demands." (*Financial Times* Leader 23 May 1994). The Association however proposes incorporation as a solution which would mean that the large audit firms could obtain limited liability company status to gain some protection against bankruptcy (Hutton 1994).

A development along these lines is taking place in the US where, during the latter half of 1994, all the big six UK-based accounting firms are converting themselves into limited liability partnerships (LLPs) registered in the state of Delaware but now legally recognised in all other US states. LLP status protects the personal assets of partners not directly involved in work resulting in litigation. It does not protect firms' assets nor those of partners or employees directly involved in such work (Welch 1994b). At the same time (late 1994) one of the "big six", KPMG Peat Marwick, has expressed an intention to pursue incorporation for its audit arm and has begun canvassing clients. Kelly (1994) argues that despite the disclosure requirements of company accounts, coupled with an increased tax burden on partners, this pioneering course of action appears to provide KPMG with a distinct market edge, in particular because it will enable them to demonstrate their ability to withstand the effects of sizeable claims.

The DTI is clearly faced with a dilemma. Doing nothing might appeal to those who see the ICAEW's case as being based on protecting the very profitable interests of the big firms, but it is possible that, without protection, they may begin to turn away high risk clients or raise fees significantly to cover costs (Jack 1994a). Further, Hatherly (1989) suggests that if litigation damages continue to spiral upwards, together with premiums for indemnity insurance, the auditor's role might change in that he would be effectively insuring third party users for the reliability of their financial statements. This may alter the auditor's responsibility for collecting audit evidence to support his opinion. The effect might be that he would collect evidence to the extent that its cost was less than the associated reduction in insurance premium, that is to say, a trade-off between insurance costs and audit thoroughness, making audit reports little more than insurance certificates. This clearly represents a threat to audit quality. It would appear that, with a possible further Companies Act in 1995 or 1996, the balance of argument may sway the government to act and allow contractual capping.

A further consequence of inaction might be that companies are obliged to pay for professional indemnity insurance for their auditors in order to persuade them to act as their auditors. Such an arrangement was discussed at the AGM of Unilever in 1994 in a scheme to enable the arrangement of insurance for their directors and "officers", including auditors. This can only serve to add to the costs of audit and to reduce its independence. The Unilever Board are now empowered to proceed with this if they so decide (*Accountancy Age* 12 May 1994).

Conclusion

If the issue presents the government with a dilemma in the UK, the strength of the campaign for reform is much greater in the USA and Australia. In the US, where the campaign is aimed at changing joint and several liability law to one of proportionate liability, a bill has been placed before the US House of Representatives. In Australia, the Attorney General in February 1994 asked a professor of law and a judge to examine the case for change. It should be noted that Germany already has a legal limit to liability of almost £$^1/_4$m. Perhaps in the UK the case was weakened by the Caparo decision, but the size of international claims against UK-based firms continues to grow (Jack 1994a; *Accountancy Age* 21 April 1994). Claims against Price Waterhouse and Ernst Young over BCCI now exceed £8bn whilst Touche Ross face a £1bn suit over Atlantic Computers, the failed client of Spicer and Pegler, taken over by Touche in 1990. The case for reform can no longer be ignored, even in the UK, where the government may well be induced to act in part by threats to its audit firms and measures taken to protect them elsewhere in the world.

Table of Cases

Al Saudi Bank and others v Clark Pixley and another (1990) 2 WLR 344; (1989) 3 All ER 361

Berg Sons and Co and others v Adams and others (1992) Queens Bench Divisional (Commercial Court)

Candler v Crane Christmas (1951) 2 KP 164; (1951)1 All ER 361

Caparo Industries PLC v Dickman and others (1990) HL (E)

Galoo and others v Bright Grahame and Murray (1993)

Hedley Byrne and Co Ltd v Heller and Partners Ltd (1964) AC 465 (HL)(E)

James McNaughton Paper Group Ltd v Hicks Anderson and Co (1991) 1 All ER 134

Jeb Fasteners Ltd v Marks Bloom and Co (1981) 3 All ER 289

Re Kingston Cotton Mill Co Ltd (No2) (1896) 2 Ch 279

Lloyd Cheyham v Littlejohn (1985) BCLC

Morgan Crucible Co PLC v Hill Samuel and Co Ltd (1990) 3 All ER 330; (1991) 1 All ER 148 (CA)

Re Thomas Gerrard and Sons Ltd (1968) Ch4 55

Twomax Ltd v Dickson, McFarlane and Robinson (1982) Sc 113.

References

Accountancy Age (1994) Editorials. 10 March, 21 April, 12 May

Arnheim, A. (1991) "Auditors" Fate in the Crucible?" *Accountancy,* Vol 107, Iss 1173, May, p94–95

Auditing Practices Board (1992) "The Future Development of Auditing" APB Green Paper

Auditing Practices Committee (1983) "Attendance at Stocktaking" APC Auditing Guideline, para 5

Baker, N. (1994a) "DTI told to Cap Liability', and "Audit Liability Campaign shifts to Public Interest" *Accountancy Age* 3 February

Baker, N. (1994b) "Big Six dealt blow over liability plea", and "Audit Liability debate splits Institute Council" *Accountancy Age* 10 March

Bartlett, R.W.(1994) " 'Fairness' revisited : Does Rule 203 help or hurt?" Research paper to be published – presented to the Liverpool Business School, Liverpool John Moores University October 1994 by Prof. Bartlett, California State University.

Committee on the Financial Aspects of Corporate Governance (1992) *The Cadbury Report* Gee & Co Ltd

Dunn, J. (1991) *Auditing – Theory and Practice,* Prentice Hall

The Economist (1994) "If the Cap fits" 26 February

Financial Times (1994) leader, 23 May.

Gwillian, D. (1985) "Negligence – a legal attitude" *Accountancy* September p80

Hatherly, D. (1989) "Audit reports or insurance certificates?" *Accountancy* May pp27–28

Hoskins, M. (1993) "The future of Auditing – a Big Six view" *Accountancy (ACE)* Vol 111, Iss 1198 June 1993 p88

Humphrey,C. Mozier,P., Turley,S. (1993) "The audit expectations gap in Britain – an empirical investigation" *Accounting & Business Research* Vol 23, Iss 91A, 1993 pp395–411

Hutton, B. (1994) "Warning on cap to audit liability" *Financial Times* 25 April

ICAEW (1965) "Accountants' Liability to Third Parties" *ICAEW* Statement V8

Jack, A. (1994a) "Grab for a Lifebelt" *Financial Times* 25 February

Jack, A. (1994b) "Accountants split over liability cap", *Financial Times* 10 March

Jack, A. (1994c) "Crying wolf too often over the liability crisis" *Financial Times* 16 June

Jack, A. (1994d). "Caparo–Touche saga ends with a twist in the tail" *Financial Times* 4 August

Keenan, D. (1983) "Professional Negligence up to date" *Accountancy* February pp62–64

Keenan, D. (1989) "Auditor's duty of care" *Accountancy* October pp46–48

Kelly,J. (1994) "Opening the books and limiting liability" *Financial Times* 13 October 1994

Lee, T. (1992) "The Audit Liability Crisis – they protest too much!" *Accountancy* December p102

Likierman, A. (1989) "Professional Liability – report of the study teams", HMSO

Luscombe,N. (1993) "A threat to our health" *CA Magazine* Vol 126, Iss 9 October 1993 p3

Mitchell,A., Puxty,A., Sikka,P., Willmott,H. (1994) "The Auditor Liability Charade" University of East London

O'Sullivan, N. (1993). "Auditors' Liability: Its role in the corporate governance debate" *Accounting and Business Research* Vol 23, Iss 91A, pp412–420

Paskell Mede, M. (1990) "Duty's not in the eye of the beholder" *CA Magazine*, Vol123, Iss 4 April pp29–31

Penn, G. (1991) "The Courts – Liability of auditors to third parties' *Banking World*, Vol9, Iss2 February p55

Pounds, G.D. and Courtis,J.K. (1980) "The Auditors' Liability – a myth?" *Accounting and Business Research* Summer pp299–305

Pratt, M.J. (1982) *Auditing*, Longmans (2nd Ed)

Savage, N. (1981) "The Auditor's legal responsibility – to strangers?" *Accountants' Magazine* October pp338–341

Singleton Green, B. (1990) "Limiting Auditors' Liability" *Accountancy* Vol 6, Iss 1163 July pp97–97

Weekly Law Reports (1990) 23 February pp358–407

Welch, I. (1994a) "JMU report rocks audit liability lobby" *Accountancy Age* 10 February

Welch, I. (1994b) "Limited liability by US Big Six" *Accountancy Age* 18 August

Wise, L. (1994) "There but for the grace of God" *Accountancy Age* 17 February

Woolf, E. (1994) *Auditing Today,* Prentice Hall (5th Ed).

3

International Accounting

Roger Pegum

Introduction

The globalisation of financial activity has dramatically increased the significance of the variations in accounting practice across different countries. Differences in compilation and interpretation are of fundamental significance to the world's financial markets and have led to increased efforts to harmonise accounting practice.

In order to identify the main areas of divergence, a number of studies have been undertaken. Cooke (1992) identified three categories of European policy issues for consideration depending upon whether they were of direct, indirect or marginal concern. She identified the general strategy pursued by accountancy bodies which was one of seeking to influence legislation and, where necessary, lobbying against ineffective legislation.

Al Hashim and Arpan (1988) analysed the extent to which accounting regulations in Europe had their origins in legislation, professional body requirements, or both. They identified a UK/US/Dutch model of considerable professional involvement in regulation; a French model where the profession prepares legislation but only makes non-mandatory recommendations; and a German model where the profession is concerned with compliance.

Nobes (1991) contrasted the "common law" tradition, which avoided prescription of a large number of detailed all-embracing rules, with the codified Roman Law which established rules in detail for accounting and financial reporting. The former tradition clearly left room for a substantial professional role in policy formation. This is reflected in the individual professional bodies of the UK, Ireland and the Netherlands and the significant influence of the representative body, the Federation des Experts Comptables (FEE), against which the European Commission has sought to ensure independence through the creation of the Accounting Forum.

Irvine (1992) chronicled the difficulties in reaching any conclusions in the European Accounting Forum and highlighted the development of "comitology" as the means by which the European Commission could ignore the deliberations of the representative and National bodies and formulate its own policy.

These international differences in the formation of accounting policy are significant and may be considered alongside, for instance, the treatment of taxation in financial reporting where the UK and US approach ignores the calculation of taxation in published accounts reflecting the separate rules that apply to such calculations compared to those applicable to published statements. The use of fixed capital allowances (accelerated depreciation) rather than judgemental depreciation for taxation purposes is a case in point. France, Germany, Italy and Spain treat published accounts as the basis for taxation.

Within the context of the differences outlined above, this chapter examines the main developments in international accounting and the main areas of controversy.

Religion and Accounting
There are important cultural influences on accounting and business practice, perhaps the most important being religion. Religion results in a particular ethical environment within which business is conducted and its impact upon accounting practice is often overlooked.

Shaari, Craig and Clarke (1993) discussed the contrast between developed countries, with their neo-colonial links, and Islamic countries. They recognised the leading role of the US, linked to Japan and the Phillipines, and the UK, linked to India, Singapore, Malaysia, Hong Kong and others. They recognised that the accounting practices common to the above arose from Judaic-Christian philosophy and the Protestant work ethic. Their emphasis lay with the role of work as a virtuous activity which, as organisations developed, required reporting mechanisms to meet the needs of principals in monitoring their appointed agents, assisted by auditing experts. This contrasts with the Islamic approach to business which reflects a particularly strong ethical basis to all aspects of individual behaviour and places particular emphasis upon the need for the individual to relate his conduct to God. This manifests itself in the attitude to possessions. These are held in stewardship, in trust for others to benefit as well as oneself. All activity must be in accordance with the Holy Writ – Koran and Sunnah. All business is undertaken with justice, goodwill and honesty as paramount requirements in contrast to a Western "All's fair in Business" attitude. Muslims believe in investment but not speculation. They also attribute an enhanced role to partnerships in business practice involving the contribution of finance, labour and/or capital. A finance partnership is formed with cash as equity which avoids disputes over valuation of contributions. A labour partnership involves the agreement to a share of rewards at the beginning based upon the work to be undertaken. A credit partnership focuses upon the pledge of reputation or support to a project thereby giving it status to command further support. Partnership agreements are established on the basis of complete equality of personal status, capital and/or share of profits.

The ethical framework governing these activities is perceived to be so strong that the reporting and monitoring mechanisms common in the West appear intrusive or even insulting. This fundamental cultural difference creates significant obstacles to harmonisation in the absence of clear understanding of the different priorities of a substantial proportion of the world's population. The scandals concerning Western companies' accounting deficiencies hardly support the argument that Western practice should be adopted globally.

True and Fair View
The UK and US approach to accounting is based upon the need to meet users' decision-making requirements. This involves a perception of what is relevant for this purpose, produced with sufficient reliability to give a "true and fair view" of a company's affairs at a particular date. This forms the basis for the auditor's report and has been accepted as a fundamental part of the Fourth EC Directive. The UK perspective is based upon the perception that investors are the primary user group requiring comparability as a benchmark for choice among alternative securities.

The major problem that arises from this is the lack of a clear definition of a true and fair view. The expectation of the user would include a presentation that is clear, distinct and free from bias, fraud and injustice. The lack of user understanding concerning the level of subjectivity used in the preparation of accounts in the UK has contributed to the widely researched "Audit

Expectations Gap" as discussed by Humphrey, Moizer and Turley (1992) (See Chapter Four).

The EU Fourth Directive not only required the preparation of accounts so as to represent a True and Fair View but also required the overriding of regulations if it is necessary to meet such a requirement. The Directive has been adopted by member states but the process of translation and implementation has varied considerably in fitting the requirements into a linguistic and regulatory context. David Alexander (1993) stated that although

> True and Fair View (TFV) is an undefinable and flexible construct (i.e.will o' the wisp), which in a sense it is, and therefore as unimportant which it is not. First, it exists in law. Second, different perceptions of its meaning and significance are symptomatic of different cultural, legal and accounting attitudes and perceptions. If European accounting harmonisation is going to progress sufficiently to be able to make its proper contribution to the "level playing field" of the Single Market, then such differences must be fully exposed and discussed.

Alexander also discusses the translation of the Fourth Directive into English and German with respect to TFV and comments that: "viewed word by word, the German version and the English version are in no way direct translations; viewed as a whole, with appropriate stylistic licence, from this author's British perspective, the two versions do not appear to say the same thing". He also reviewed the French approach in which there are three separate requirements – statements must be regular, sincere and give a true image. In particular, he discussed the possibility of being regular and sincere without giving a true image which is in sympathy with the notion of a true and fair override. However, the major source of guidance in practical accounting in France, Memento Pratique Lefevbre Comptable, suggests that accounts could be established which are in accordance with regulation (regulier) and in good faith (sincere) thus giving a true and fair view. This seems to amend the approach above reducing the requirement from three to two. The further explanations in the book emphasise the theme of following regulations or established procedures rather than the pursuit of the true and fair view as a concept to avoid a wide diversity of conclusions. Alexander further describes how the British have systematically overridden the Directive through SSAP 19 on Investment Properties, SSAP 20 on Foreign Currency Translation and SSAP 9 on Stocks and Work in Progress.

The Directive does not allow for properties to be shown at valuation and not depreciated. It also does not allow unrealised profits as in foreign currency translation gains and estimated profits on long-term contracts as is justified in the pursuit of a TFV in the UK.

Ordelheide (1993) contends that the "true and fair principle of the Fourth Directive is an autonomous European norm". He accepts the differences that Alexander identifies but argues that this "does not change the legal quality of the true and fair view principle of the Fourth Directive as a European accounting principle." He looks to the detailed requirements of the Directive as to what the norm represents. "An accounting method which complies with them is – irrespective of exceptional cases – in accordance with the general norm". This general norm is "the European true and fair principle with its content essentially characterised by continental European valuation standards".

He makes it clear that the essential themes of the Directive should be followed even where the Directive makes no mention of such items reflecting upon treating unrealised foreign currency translation gains as income and not depreciating investment properties seem in clear breach of the Directive or reasonable interpretations thereof. He also discusses the use of notes to convert a set of accounts prepared following accepted practice within the law in Germany to meet true and fair requirements under the Directive. He does not accept that the accounts have to be amended to meet this requirement but that the notes should be seen as part of the composite whole of the accounts to which the Directive applies.

A similar picture emerges with respect to French accounting as discussed by Burlaud (1993). He refers to the French Commercial Code which states that the "supplementary information should be provided in the notes to the accounts" without any other choices available. He also agrees with Alexander that the true and fair view is a useful concept only where the rules are insufficient or misleading, but in those cases it provides an overriding principle. He particularly emphasises the usefulness of the true and fair concept as a guide for standard setters rather than for businesses who follow the accounting rules.

Karel van Hulle (1993) said that the flexibility of interpretation of meaning of TFV

is highly desirable in an international context because of the socio-economic, cultural and legal differences between member states. It is therefore perfectly possible that annual accounts which are regarded as true and fair in one member state would not be interpreted as such in another member state.

He concurred with Alexander "that an interpretation of the true and fair override which would limit its application to disclosure in the notes is not in conformity with the wording and direction of the Directive". He also quotes the 1992 FEE Survey covering 400 companies in 15 European countries revealing that only 10 companies departed from national law to show a true and fair view. He also considered that most of these cases "would, in my view, not even qualify as a true and fair override, because the practice is explicitly allowed under the law (and the Directives)."

The Role of the Capital Markets
The dependence on equity capital of the US and UK is reflected in the listing of more than 2000 domestic companies on the stock exchanges. Germany depends upon close involvement by banks as lenders and equity shareholders. France and Italy have a long tradition of greater state intervention and close links with banks who will obtain internal information and, in Italy especially, more companies are family businesses. These characteristics lead to very different pressures for disclosure. The influence of the capital markets in the adoption of US GAAP has been seen in the need for European (other than UK) multinational companies to seek access to wider sources of finance. The traditional sources for such companies have been banks and private investors. They can no longer satisfy the requirements hence the need to gain access to international capital markets. The creation of simplified listing procedures has enabled European companies to gain multiple listings more easily. This has resulted in capital markets competing to attract such companies and the companies having to consider how to prepare their financial statements. The result has been two sets of statements, one for the domestic market and another for the foreign capital market. If the foreign market is the largest of all, the US market, then the Securities and Exchange Commission (SEC) insists upon the adoption of US GAAP.

Daimler-Benz was the first German company to register with the SEC and the translation of their accounts to US GAAP revealed the extent of disharmony in accounting practice. The company's registration document included a German GAAP/US GAAP net income reconciliation statement, which revealed that a DM158m profit under German GAAP for the six months to 30 June 1993 was, in fact, a US GAAP loss of DM949m. This was in contrast to the popular belief that German accounting is always a prudent view. It highlights the need for greater effort in the harmonisation debate.

There is a danger that US GAAP will be adopted in the absence of further progress in this debate where nationalistic perspectives create obstacles to understanding and reasonable negotiation. The focus upon harmonisation as a problem for multi-national companies rather than companies operating largely within national boundaries would assist considerably in reducing resistance to further progress given that the vast majority of companies are not interested in listing on the international capital markets. There is also considerable concern about the quality of regulation in the capital markets outside the USA in the absence of an equivalent to the SEC.

Influences on the Standard Setting Process

The Accounting Standards Board in the UK has sought to meet some of this criticism by a demonstrably rigorous approach to standard setting in the US mould with the capacity to enforce compliance. In a European context, however, it seems to be working in isolation in many respects. The creation of a pan-European regulatory body would seem to be an appropriate response to demonstrate the quality of monitoring underpinning the markets to rival the US. It is likely that European multi-nationals will seek US listing in the absence of such measures to secure the position of the European role in world financing (Wilson 1994). The continuing development of international standards through the International Accounting Standards Committee (IASC) subsequently endorsed in part by the International Organisation of Securities Commissions (IOSCO) has placed particular pressure upon the EC Commission to adopt these standards for its members but this has been resisted as inappropriate for many countries.

The IASC consists of representatives of approximately 100 professional bodies from 80 countries delegating standard setting to a Board of 17 members from both developed and developing countries and user groups. It has no means of enforcing its standards but IOSCO endorsement has certainly lent considerable weight to its pronouncements.

Recent experience of the continuing discussions between IASC and IOSCO has been less harmonious as the speech given by the IASC chairman at the 1994 IOSCO Conference (reported in *Accountancy* November 1994 p18) made clear. He said that IOSCO's approach to international accounting standards was deeply flawed and should be changed since it runs counter to moves, supported by IOSCO itself, towards international harmonisation. This followed IOSCO's refusal to adopt the 24 IASC Standards on its agreed list of core standards until 10 of them had been amended to its satisfaction. He looked for the 14 accepted standards to be adopted immediately. He identified IOSCO's approach as "unsatisfactory" for a number of reasons.

First, it ignores the substantial improvements in financial reporting that flow from the use of IAS's. It also means that the financial statements of world class European companies that conform with national requirements, European Union Directives and IAS's are unacceptable for IOSCO even though they are acceptable for domestic regulators. Second, IOSCO seems to expect more of the IASC than it does of national standard-setting bodies in expecting resolution of matters not yet resolved at national level. An example concerns the need for an IAS on capital instruments before it will accept the core standards but the US FASB has not yet produced a standard on this. Third, IOSCO is reviewing each IAS in detail and only accepting those which meet domestic criteria. This was felt to represent a move against international harmonisation by allowing reinstatement of options previously ruled out and treatments considered unacceptable by the IASC.

The considerable difference between the volumes of shares traded on major exchanges like London and New York and on smaller exchanges like Frankfurt and Paris is reflected in the information requirements of such users in those countries (Ballweiser 1991).

It must be recognised that the globalisation of markets has led to institutional investors, particularly from the US and Japan, investing in these smaller markets and, possibly, exploiting the less-demanding regulatory regimes. IOSCO is addressing this as above and the EU has implemented the Seventh Directive requiring consolidation of group results so that a fairer picture is obtained. This has had a particular impact in Germany where companies reported and were taxed on an individual basis until 1990 and foreign subsidiaries were not consolidated.

The Seventh Directive was largely based upon UK practice as it is the only EU country with extensive experience in accounting for acquisitions and mergers. Since its adoption in 1983, the Seventh Directive has been seen to include a wide variety of options to meet the needs of member states. It has been successful in implementing the requirement for full consolidation of subsidiary's results in group accounts and the recognition of investments as providers of income and valued at the lower of cost and net realisable value in the balance sheet. It has been less successful in the harmonious treatment of associates through equity accounting and accounting for joint ventures. In its adoption of UK practice the Seventh Directive has inherited certain perceived weaknesses especially the ability to capitalise reorganisation costs of subsidiaries, create provisions for losses and write down the value of assets acquired on takeover. These matters have been addressed in FRS 7 applicable from December 1994 by not allowing these costs to be used to reduce the fair value of assets acquired in calculating goodwill on acquisition. They will have to be written off post acquisition through the P/L account.

The controversy surrounding the publication of this standard, especially the dissenting vote of the user representative on the ASB and the reaction of the 100 Group of Financial Directors of large companies, is interesting. It remains to be seen who prevails in this discussion but the editorial in the November 1994 issue of *Accountancy* has supported the view of the ASB. The industrialists' argument is based upon the idea that reorganisation costs are part of the total cost of the acquisition and therefore ought to be capitalised. The editorial makes clear that unless reorganisation costs were incurred as part of the acquisition, they should be treated as revenue. Consideration would have to be given as to whether they are extraordinary items in the light of stricter definitions of these matters in FRS 3. They should not be treated as capital unless they fall within normal understanding of the term such as expenditure on fixed assets. The argument put forward by industrialists is further criticised because of the desire to deduct the reorganisation and other costs in arriving at the fair value of the net assets acquired rather than normal depreciation or amortisation. The resulting enhancement of goodwill would be written off against reserves under SSAP 22 rather than through the P/L. This avoids charging these costs against income at all. Smith (1992) described this as "probably the area of acquisition accounting which has provided the greatest opportunity for abuse."

Brunovs and Kirsch (1991) identified the impact that the adoption of IAS 22 would have by pointing out the mismatch between its requirement for amortisation of goodwill over five years rather than the UK approach or the practice in the US and elsewhere of adopting amortisation periods of 20 to 40 years. They also identified the problems of the treatment of reorganisation costs and the lack of comparability that results from the UK's approach. They made this point clearly.

> The inconsistency between standards in relation to (these) issues has two financial reporting consequences. First, the UK standard provides the opportunity for inherently conservative calculations in the highly subjective area of estimating future reorganisation costs to be incorporated in the calculation of goodwill on acquisition. This may result in the increase of goodwill which is to be immediately written off against reserves. As a consequence costs and expenses which may in all other circumstances be charged against revenue in the income statement could be charged against reserves. Second, UK companies' future earnings are not penalised by amortisation charges when the direct write-off approach is applied. On the other hand, those countries which require systematic amortisation of goodwill over time may place resident companies at a competitive

disadvantage in acquisition activity vis-a-vis UK companies since the non-UK companies must be concerned about the impact of future goodwill charges against future period's earnings. Thus, non-UK companies may not be able to offer as much in competitive bidding.

This view is further supported by Daniel Ivancevich (1993) who found that

the results of the study indicate there is a difference in the amount of premiums paid in acquisitions of US targets between US and UK buyers. The goodwill variable tested proved to be significant in both the short- and long-term databases. The explanation for this significance is the differences which exist in the accounting for purchased goodwill in the US and UK. In view of these findings, perhaps it is appropriate to suggest that the FASB re-examine its current position on the accounting for purchased goodwill.

The US is less likely to change than the UK which is out of step on these matters and is likely to change when the ASB discussion paper on goodwill published in December 1993 has received full consideration. This paper put forward four approaches with two of them preferred by at least some of the ASB's members. In the paper the ASB point out that, since 1976, the amount paid for goodwill as a percentage of the acquirer's net worth pre-acquisition had grown from 1% to 44% in 1987. The ASB stated that moves away from the write off against reserves had begun with the Urgent Issues Task Force Abstract 3, which concluded that goodwill should be charged to the P/L account on the ultimate closure or disposal of the related business. The old Accounting Standards Committee issued ED 47 just before its demise which would have put the UK in line with most other countries by requiring the capitalisation and amortisation of goodwill over its useful economic life, usually 20 years. The ASB paper says that accounting for purchased intangibles is so closely related to the purchased goodwill question that "most purchased intangible assets should be subsumed within purchased goodwill for reporting purposes". The current ban on recognising non-purchased or inherent goodwill should remain. The ASB still favour the ED 47 approach allowing, exceptionally, for goodwill with an economic life greater than 20 years to be subject to a formal annual recoverability review with "ceiling" tests to determine an appropriate depreciation charge. A separate goodwill write-off reserve would be established where it would remain untouched unless the related business was closed or disposed of. The responses to this discussion paper were mixed and the question is not yet resolved for the UK.

Companies are faced with difficult decisions on determining which

Standards to adopt since considerable expense is clearly involved as well as a consciousness of the users for whom the information is intended. The IASC has sought to address the differences available under its Standards by issuing Exposure Draft 32 on Comparability of Financial Statements in 1989. This stated that variations in treatment would be considered in the light of its "Framework for the Preparation and Presentation of Financial Statements" also issued in 1989. E32 covered 29 issues in 13 Standards where options exist for alternative treatments of like events. It indicates preferred options, those it is prepared to allow and those it will not allow. In inventory valuation it prefers FIFO or Weighted Average, allows LIFO but does not allow base stock. The influence of US GAAP may play a large part in the retention of LIFO.

Harmonisation, Mutual Recognition or Diversity of Accounting Practice
It is now appropriate to study the treatment of different items in the accounts in different countries. The differing approach followed by multinationals using the IASC requirements in anticipation of national regulations is apparent; they do so as part of a public relations process of being seen to adopt the highest standards and to meet stock exchange requirements (Archer and McLeay 1992).

Goodwill on consolidation has been discussed at length already but offers interesting contrasts following the long debate in the UK with no provision being made in France, Finland, Sweden and Norway for write off against reserves (the prevalent practice).

The treatment of depreciation depends very much on whether it is used for tax purposes as in Belgium, France (but not to consolidated accounts), Germany and Portugal. The straight line method is the most common, though reducing balance is popular in France and Germany as accelerated depreciation is allowable for tax purposes.

Revaluation of land and buildings is allowed in half the EU Countries. It is not adopted in Germany but is especially widespread in Ireland, Italy, Spain and the UK. Italy bases its view on legal requirements whereas the UK pursues the true and fair view.

On the valuation of inventory, 52% of companies in Germany and 72% in Italy use LIFO reflecting the tax position in contrast to explicit prohibition in the UK.

The valuation of long-term contracts is generally by percentage of completion but the completed contract method is wholly used in Germany and 50% in France.

Foreign currency translation arises as an issue whenever a company enters into transactions involving foreign currencies. It has to be decided how gains and losses on these transactions should be identified and how they should be reflected in the financial statements. A company which has foreign subsidiaries (associates or branches) needs to translate their financial statements for consolidation purposes. A distinction needs to be drawn between individual companies and consolidated accounts. In the case of the individual company, different countries sometimes distinguish between short- and long-term treatment. The UK, France and the Netherlands make no distinction whereas IAS 21 (reflecting US practice), Germany and Spain do make such distinctions. The other major issue affecting the individual company concerns the recognition of gains or losses. All recognise losses on translation immediately but half recognise unrealised gains (Denmark, Ireland, UK and Netherlands) while others carry forward (France, Germany and Greece). Belgium, Luxembourg, Italy and Spain are undecided. It has proved to be a difficult issue having been omitted from the Fourth and Seventh Directives but there is a relatively high degree of harmony of practice in the EU. This seems to follow from a widespread acceptance of IAS 21 which is broadly in line with FAS 52 and from a desire to minimise the impact of volatile exchange rates on profits.

It must also be accepted that the level of foreign exchange risk now experienced is much greater but this is not reflected in accounts. Policies on hedging can remove much of this risk.

The inconsistency in treatment of these matters occurs at both the individual and consolidated levels of accounts. At the individual level, there is inconsistency in the treatment of short- and long-term monetary items. A recent survey published by Samuels, Brayshaw and Craner (1994) identified the UK, France and the Netherlands as having no difference between the treatment of short- or long-term monetary items while IAS 21 (and US practice), Germany and Spain do make such a distinction. Individual companies in these countries vary even more in their recognition of gains and/or losses. This may include the recognition of all gains and losses (UK), with short-term treated differently to long-term by deferring long-term gains and losses and recognising them in current and future income on a systematic basis.

Further complexity of treatment applies to other countries making harmonisation difficult. For consolidated accounts the vast majority apply the closing rate method in their balance sheets according to the survey referred to above with a minority of companies in Germany applying the temporal method. In the profit and loss account 57% use a historical rate with the closing rate making up the majority of the remainder. Many multinational companies make use of currency options or futures contracts to limit the impact of exchange rate fluctuations on overseas profits. Few companies in Europe outside the UK provide information on the policies used. This is an area for development in accounting regulation.

Considerable differences in reported profits can result from the adoption of different standards. British Telecom (BT) reported profits for the year ended 31 March 1994 of £1,767m under UK GAAP but this was revised to £1,476m under US GAAP – a reduction of 16.5% and shareholders' equity fell from £13,026m to £11,511m – a reduction of 11.6%. As the US and UK represent relatively tightly regulated reporting environments the differences elsewhere are likely to be considerable.

An interesting study by the Centre for International Financial Analysis (1993) restated the accounts of companies from eight different countries using standards representing "best practice." They identified the following changes to net income:

Changes to Net Income: Effect of Restatement to Common Standards

	%
Sweden	+60
Germany	+44
Japan	+12
Italy	+11
Belgium	+ 9
France	+ 6
UK	+ 4
Switzerland	− 8

They particularly focused upon the treatment of tangible fixed assets and goodwill as major causes of difference between the countries' implementation of standards. Differences in disclosure practices adds to the difficulties in performing these sorts of comparisons with Switzerland, in particular, presenting a limited view of the determination of net income.

Multinational companies are subject to a variety of regulatory frameworks with differing measurement, disclosure and auditing requirements. They would clearly benefit from a greater degree of harmonisation.

On the basis of this it seems that the Fourth Directive requirement that accounts across the EC should show a "true and fair view" has led to less harmonisation as options are exercised especially in companies operating solely in that country. Alexander and Archer (1992) argue that the process was begun from a diverse base with the need to distinguish the difference between the presentational level and the content, valuation and attitudinal levels in European financial reporting.

References

Accounting Standards Board (1993) *Discussion Paper on Goodwill* December

Al Hashim, D. Arpan, J. (1988) *International Dimensions of Accounting* PWS Kent

Alexander, D. (1993) "A European True and Fair View?" *European Accounting Review*

Alexander, D. and Archer G.S.H. (1992) (Eds) *The European Accounting Guide* Academic Press

Archer, G.S.H. and McLeay S (1992) *European Financial Reporting* in Student Financial Reporting 1991–1992 ICAEW

Ballweiser, H. (1991) Paper on the German approach to Financial reporting given at European Accounting Workshop, Oxford

Burlaud Alain (1993) Commentary on the article by David Alexander "A European True and Fair View" *European Accounting Review*

Brunovs, R. and Kirsch, R.J. (1991) "Goodwill Accounting in Selected Countries and the Harmonisation of International Accounting Standards" *Abacus* Vol 27 No2

Centre for International Financial Analysis (1993) *International Accounting and Auditing Trends* CIFA

Cooke, R. (1992) "Influence in the Community" *Accountancy* July pp 86–7

Humphrey, C. G., Moizer, P. and Turley, S. (1992) *The Audit Expectations Gap in the United Kingdom* London, The Research Board, ICAEW

Irvine, J. (1992) "European Accounting Forum: Hidden Agenda?" *Accountancy* June pp22–3

Ivancevich, D. M. (1993) "Acquisitions and Goodwill:The United Kingdom and the United States" *International Journal of Accounting*

Nobes, C. and Parker R. (1991) *Comparative International Accounting* Prentice Hall

Ordelheide, D. (1993) "True and Fair View, A European and German Perspective" *European Accounting Review*

Samuels, J. M., Brayshaw R. E. and Craner J. M. (1994) *Financial Statement Analysis in Europe* Chapman and Hall

Shaari, H., Craig R. and Clarke F. (1993) "Religion: A Confounding

Cultural Element in the International Harmonisation of Accounting"
Abacus Vol 29 No2

Smith, T. (1992) *Accounting for Growth* Century Business

Van Hulle, K. (1993) "Truth and Untruth about true and fair: a
commentary on 'A European true and fair view' " *European Accounting
Review*

Wilson, A. (1994) "Harmonisation: Is it now or never for Europe?"
Accountancy November p98

4

Internal Audit – Perceptions of Quality and the Expectations Gap within a Competitive Environment

Bob Hopkins and Ken Purnell

Introduction

Internal audit is defined in the Auditing Practices Committee (APC) (1990 para 1) guidelines as

> an independent appraisal function established by the management of an organisation for the review of the internal control system as a service to the organisation. It objectively examines, evaluates and reports on the adequacy of internal control as a contribution to the proper, economic, efficient and effective use of resources.

An "expectation gap" can be described as the difference between what you want to happen and what actually happens.

In the developing competitive market for internal audit services it is the managers within an organisation who are responsible for purchasing the audit services provided by the internal audit function. The purchasing of any service implies that some assessment of the quality of that service has taken place. The risk for any audit manager is that customers' perceptions of what makes a quality service are different from those of the auditors who would provide that service. Any perceptual differences between the would-be providers and purchasers of audit services may create an expectation gap that could prejudice the success and survival of internal audit in a competitive environment.

The Chartered Institute of Public Finance and Accountancy (CIPFA) has stated that modern quality philosophy is very customer-centred and the needs and expectations of the customer are of primary importance. The major risk for any audit manager therefore is that there is no awareness of their purchasers' quality perceptions of internal audit.

This chapter is based on initial research undertaken in 1992 at Liverpool Business School and is based entirely on the public sector. The chapter will demonstrate that: there are many significant differences between the way that auditors and auditees understand the meaning of a quality audit product; the majority of these differences raise direct questions at the level of both audit and auditee management; and that they are so significant that they may compromise internal audit's ability to survive in the developing market-orientated environment.

In the developing arena of service level agreements, contractual relationships and increased competition it will be argued that, if internal audit is to offer a viable market-orientated product, it is essential to recognise that perceptual differences of internal audit currently exist.

Background

In recent years within the public sector there have been a number of changes and challenges facing the providers of traditional internal audit resulting from wider changes to the organisation and delivery of public services. There has been a swing "back to basics", fuelled by the expectations gap and recent corporate scandals and failures. As a consequence a view is developing that audit should carry out less value for money (VFM) and consultancy services and more regularity and probity work. This is already beginning to affect some public sector auditors as the Audit Commission has made an announcement that more probity work should be undertaken.

However, in order for internal audit to secure work and maximise effectiveness, it is essential that perceptual differences of internal audit are addressed. This involves a link with the concept of total quality management (TQM). For example, Hogan (1994) states that to improve the quality of internal auditing the auditor needs to determine who the customers are and also their needs. Carcello et al (1992) emphasise both the importance of understanding user perceptions as they relate to audit quality and the requirement to be responsive to client needs. This should enable internal audit to formulate a strategy to narrow or remove the expectations gap. This would in turn improve the quality of the audit process and deliver the most appropriate product for the quality-driven market environment.

In an article in the *Financial Times*, Atchley (1993) discussed the findings of recent research carried out by Kato Communications and Gilchrist Practice Development Consultants which showed that many practitioners have failed to understand client needs and attitudes. The findings are important as they purport to show that the firms that are likely to succeed in the medium term will only be those which are effective in narrowing the gap between client's expectations and client's experiences of the services provided.

Methodology

The research has centred on potential behavioural problems between auditors and auditees. It was suggested that if the auditor and the auditee perceived the meaning of "audit" in significantly different ways then there was likely to be a lack of communication occurring from the outset which could lead to an ineffective audit process. Was this why auditors were not always welcomed with open arms?

The argument was extended to include quality issues for internal audit, especially those within a competitive market. It was suggested that if there was no consensus on the meaning of the word "audit" then individuals would attach different quality ideas to the concept of internal audit and that this might have damaging consequences in a competitive situation. If internal audit is to maximise its market opportunities then it will have to be aware of any areas where differing perceptions of audit occur.

Before any research could be carried out it was necessary to consider what terms were being used to describe the audit process. A literature search was carried out to establish the key words that were being used in connection with auditing and these appeared to fall into three categories:

1. audit objectives (**O**)
2. audit activities (**A**)
3. auditor's personal qualities and skills (**S**)

The tables that follow will use the abbreviations O, A and S to represent the above three categories.

A questionnaire was devised to obtain opinion as to how strongly the key words were associated with a quality audit product and was sent to a number of public sector organisations (see below). Replies were received from both auditors and auditees at a variety of levels throughout the organisations. The questionnaire was designed to enable a large number of statistical comparisons to be carried out, although this chapter concentrates on those key issues that arise when auditors and auditees are compared on a management / non-management basis. A total of 1,397 questionnaires were returned making this survey one of the largest of its kind ever carried out within the UK public sector. The sample was obtained from 43 organisations: 21 local authorities, 18 health and 4 other. The breakdown is as follows.

Local authorities:	6 County Councils
	2 District Councils
	13 Metropolitan Authorities
Health:	3 Regional Health Authorities
	10 District Health Authorities
	3 Family Health Service Authorities
	2 Trusts
Other:	Audit Commission
	British Rail
	Department of Social Security
	North West Water

57% of respondents classified themselves as managerial and 43% as non-managerial while 24% were auditors and 76% were auditees.

Because of the large number of comparisons available some *directional tool* had to be employed to show where the major areas of difference occurred to provide a natural structure for the ensuing analysis. The natural comparisons are as follows.

1. audit managers to auditee managers
2. audit managers to audit non-managers
3. audit non-managers to auditee non-managers
4. auditee managers to auditee non-managers
5. audit managers to auditee non-managers

For each of the five groupings shown above, the mean scores of each of the 48 key words were compared to test whether any correlation existed between them. The correlation coefficients should then show how closely for example the audit managers "quality" assessment of the 48 key words matched that of the auditee managers.

Findings

A complete listing of all of the key words used in the survey is given in Appendix 1. What is surprising is the number of differences found. Some were certainly to be expected but the survey revealed that there are in fact a considerable number of significant differences. The results are shown in Table 1 below where the higher the correlation coefficient the closer the agreement of the groups concerned.

Table 1

Correlations of the Mean Scores of the Key Words

Main Comparators	Correlation
Audit managers to audit non-managers	0.96
Auditee managers to auditee non-managers	0.92
Audit non-managers to auditee managers	0.89
Audit managers to auditee mangers	0.87
All auditors to all auditees	0.85
Audit non-managers to auditee non-managers	0.78
Audit managers to auditee non-managers	0.70

The diagram may offer some comfort to the auditor as the best fit occurs between the audit manager and the audit non-managers. This is not too surprising as it could be expected that a respectable auditing empathy should exist between these two groups. However the worst fit occurs between audit managers and auditee non-managers. The extent of the problem can be seen if a calculation is made showing what percentage of the 48 key words tested show significantly different perceptions of a quality audit product. The results are shown in Table 2 below.

Table 2

Percentage of Key Terms with a Significant Difference

Comparators	Percentage
Audit managers to audit non-managers	15
Auditee managers to auditee non-managers	35
Audit managers to auditee managers	60
Audit non-managers to auditee managers	58
Audit managers to auditee non-managers	69

The table clearly demonstrates the problem. 69% of the key words tested are scored differently in a statistically significant way between audit managers and auditee non-managers.

It is argued that out of the five comparisons made there is least contact between audit managers and auditee non-managers. Some explanation of how this large expectation gap can have occurred is required. Two questions arise. First, by what route have auditee non-managers obtained their opinions on what a quality audit service actually is? Second, what are the key areas of difference?

In answer to the first question, it can be suggested from Table 2 that as there is a disturbingly high number of differences (60%) between audit managers and auditee managers that this is the *primary* source of the expectation gap. This gap is compounded by a 35% level of difference between auditee managers and non-managers.

It is contended that it is audit managers who are the most likely group to have the better perception of what a quality audit product should be. Audit managers receive advice from their professional bodies and should be well-acquainted with auditing standards and guidelines which codify quality audit practices.

The findings will be examined in three sections.

Section A   Quality perception of audit managers

Section B　　Provider versus provider – a comparison between audit managers and non-audit managers

Section C　　Key statistical differences

Section A: Quality Perceptions of Audit Managers

The first detailed results that will be examined are the highest ranking key words of the audit shown below in Table 3.

Table 3

**Audit Managers – Quality Perceptions
High Ranking Key Words**

Rank	Key Word	Type
1	Reporting	A
2	Service to Management	A
3	Professionalism	S
4	Recommend Improvements	O
5	Innovative	S
6	Objectivity	S
7	Evaluating	A
8	Advising	A
9	Sense of Responsibility	S
10	Achieve Improvements in Quality	O

The table shows that audit managers do appear to value the qualities identified in the auditing guidelines (APC 1990), seeing themselves as a "professional reporting function supporting management generally by recommending improvements through innovation". This survey-derived definition does indeed seem appropriate but there are one or two interesting words that did not make the top ten. For example *achieve value for money* and *independence* did not feature – perhaps being replaced by Achieve Improvements in Quality and Objectivity which did feature. "Independence" is a key audit concept recognised by the existence of an auditing guideline. Section 13 of the guideline brings together the two elements of *independence* and *objectivity* as follows.

> Each internal auditor should have an objective attitude of mind and be in a sufficiently independent position to be able to exercise judgement, express opinions and present recommendations with impartiality.

The significantly higher ranking of *objectivity* by both auditors and, as will be shown later, auditees clearly shows that the two key words of *independence* and *objectivity* are not synonymous and are valued quite differently in terms of audit quality. Audit managers did not seem to place a strong emphasis on any specialist skills (computer literacy for example). It is also possible to examine low-ranking key words as determined by audit managers and these are given in Table 4.

It is clear that modern audit managers reject the old historical role of auditor as the ticking, criticising, error finder. It is also interesting to note the rank position of qualifications and specialist skills.

The above findings support the work of earlier research by Morgan and Pattinson (1975) who found that auditors like the advisor image in which close working relationships are established (service to management) but contradicts Morgan and Pattinson in that they determined that auditors opt for the inspecting role as paramount. Table 4 above clearly shows a rejection of the inspecting role, ranked 45th out of 48 key words.

Section B: Provider versus Purchaser – a Comparison between Audit Managers and Non-Audit Managers
In any competitive environment where the internal audit service becomes a product that has to be sold then it can be assumed that potential purchasers of any audit product would be willing to purchase more of a product that conformed to *their* quality perceptions rather than those of the provider. Atchley (1993), considering the Kato Communications research, raised the issue that as long as the audit continues to be perceived as a low-value service, clients will want to buy as cheaply as possible. Therefore, one of the most serious challenges facing internal audit is the shift from a supply-led to a demand-led market.

Table 4

**Audit Managers Quality Perceptions
Low Ranking Key Words**

Rank	Key Word	Type
48	Ticking	A
47	Criticising	A
46	Error finding	A
45	Inspecting	A
44	Qualifications	S
43	Checking	A
42	Monitoring	A
41	Detecting	A
40	Specialist Skills	S
39	Observing	A

In the case of internal audit it will be the auditee managers who, in the main, will be the purchasers of audit services and any differences in perception between audit managers (the providers) and prospective purchasers might have dramatic consequences for the future of internal audit services. This view is supported by Johnson (1992) who considers that the primary improvement area for internal auditing is to provide quality customer service to management and that one of the strategies for achieving this aim is to learn to speak the language of the customer.

We now move on to the most vital part of the analysis – the search for any significantly different quality perceptions of internal audit between the audit manager and the auditee manager. When the top ten rankings of the audit managers are compared to the auditee manager's rankings of the same words a number of differences emerge. See Table 5.

Table 5

**Audit Management compared to auditee Management
Ranked by Mean Values**

Key Word	Auditor Ranking	Auditee Ranking	Difference
Reporting	1	12	−11
Service to Management	2	3	−1
Professionalism	3	1	2
Recommend Improvements	4	14	−10
Innovative	5	10	−5
Objectivity	6	2	4
Evaluating	7	21	−14
Advising	8	19	−11
Achieve Improvements in Quality	9	6	3
Sense of Responsibility	10	9	1

The positive results are that the auditee managers top five ranked items
appear on the same list as the audit managers. It must be encouraging to see
the correlation between the two groups for key words such as *service to
management, professionalism, achieve improvements in quality* etc. However, it is
surprising to find the audit manager's number one ranked key word *reporting*
is ranked only 12th by the auditee manager. Similarly, there are large
ranking differences between *recommending improvements, evaluating* and *advising*.
The reasons for these differences will be discussed later but for the moment
there is some reassurance for auditors to be gained from an examination of
the auditee manger's ranking of the top ten audit-quality key words. See
Table 6.

Table 6

**Auditee Management compared to Auditor Management
Ranked By Mean Values**

Key Word	Auditee Ranking	Auditor Ranking	
Professionalism	1	3	−2
Objectivity	2	6	−4
Service to Management	3	2	1
Achieve Value for Money	4	15	−11
Analytical	5	13	−8
Achieve Improvements in Quality	6	9	−3
Efficiency	7	17	−10
Reliability	8	12	−4
Sense of Responsibility	9	10	−1
Innovative	10	5	5

From the above, there is no sign of any historical/regularity role at all. There is a strong indication of the need for a professional service to management which is heavily orientated towards aspects of value-for-money as evidenced by the rankings of *achieve value for money, achieve improvements in quality, efficiency* and *innovation*.

These findings give a good indication of what the client wants (but not necessarily receives) and supports the Kato Communications research (Atchley 1993) which found that 31% of clients wanted a more proactive service, offering new ideas and using more imagination when analysing their business (*analytical* is ranked 5th out of 48 items in table 5 above).

The ranking of *analytical* is noteworthy, indicating a need for help. Gibbs (1993) when considering internal audit's role in quality initiatives thought that audit could focus on a number of areas, one of which was facilitating problem solving by others.

It is also interesting to note the absence of words such as *reporting* and *independence* which are deemed important enough for auditors to make them the subject of guidelines for internal auditing (APC 1990).

The rankings in Table 6 and the absence of *independence* can be contrasted to the views of a number of writers. Humphrey et al (1993) consider evidence that demonstrates the prevalence of independence-related attributes in assessments of the contribution and quality of (external) auditing. Perhaps *external* is the key difference here but Powell (1993) in considering the effectiveness of internal auditing states that "the auditor must be seen as independent" a position not demonstrated by the overall quality ranking given to *independence* by auditee managers in the survey presented here (32nd out of 48 key words).

In view of the ranking of *independence* the importance of *objectivity*, ranked second in Table 6, should not be overlooked. In terms of a behavioural context, it would be far more useful for a provider of audit services to sell the objectivity of internal auditing rather than its independence.

The above analysis has only concentrated on the differences between key words that are highly ranked by either the audit or auditee manager. It may well be the case that there are other significant differences between key words that are noteworthy.

Table 7 shows the most significantly different perceptions of internal audit quality where the audit manager rates the key words more highly.

It is important at this stage to postulate some theory as to why these particular key words appear in Table 7. These differences are so significant that the audit manager is effectively using the word in a different quality sense from the auditee manager who may take the quality meaning of these words in a completely dissimilar way.

An auditor should have no problems recognising the importance of reporting to management the results of any audit activity – this would seem to follow naturally from any reasonable definition of the internal audit process. Any quality-driven audit activity should lead to a quality audit product part of which relates to the audit report (as recognised by APC 1990).

The primary objectives of a report are:

1. to alert management to any significant matters;
2. to persuade management to implement recommendations for change;
3. to provide a formal record of points raised.

Table 7

Audit Managers Compared to Auditor Managers

Key Word	t-value
Reporting	12.0
Reliability	9.0
Recommended Improvements	8.8
Service to Management	8.5
Evaluating	8.4
Obtain Assurance	7.4
Interviewing	7.3
Innovative	7.0
Advising	6.3
Testing	5.4

On the face of it, these objectives seem innocuous. However, although reporting objectives do not have to acknowledge the behavioural consequences of the reporting function – these being inferred from other audit guidelines – it can be seen that part of the differences in perception of the reporting function are explicable by the fact that auditees subjectively evaluate the process and its consequences as discussed below.

Our research shows that auditee managers do not see the audit process in an objective fashion. By personalising the audit activities of *evaluating, obtain assurance* and *testing*, often through an "interview type" of contact, the auditee appears to feel under scrutiny with the audit report by implication raising issues that relate to personal integrity, etc.

The above is a sufficiently negative view of the audit process but Table 7 appears to show that auditee managers link the reporting process to *recommending improvements* – which signals *change*. The *innovative* skills of the auditor may also be associated with a quality audit product by auditee managers and this clearly supports the view that auditee managers see the audit process as rated by the audit manager as a process of change with potential personal consequences – not seen in any positive, quality-related way.

If audit managers are using any of the key words from Table 7 in a positive attempt to sell the internal audit services, the very use of these words may have the opposite effect from the one intended.

Section C: Key Statistical Comparisons
It is also possible to apply the t-tests to show the most significant differences in key words where the auditee managers are giving far higher quality weightings to the words than are the audit managers. The importance of these key differences shown in Table 8 are that when auditee managers are using these words they are attaching a far higher quality rating to the word than is the audit manager and this may lead to the situation where there is a lack of effective communication between the auditor and auditee because of perceptual differences of auditing quality. Indeed there can be no doubt as to the historical/probity view of auditing expressed in the differences shown in Table 8.

It must be disappointing for anyone who would support and advocate a healthy, positive audit image to find that auditee managers, in terms of a quality perception of the audit process, value *error finding, detecting, checking, ticking, preventing fraud* and *ensuring legality* far more significantly than the auditor – these being inexorably linked to the historical, regulatory function of audit. The findings are consistent with the research by Morgan and Pattinson (1975) who found that auditees view the auditor as an inspector, seeking out potential frauds and maintaining a fairly distant relationship.

Summary
The research has shown that there is an expectation gap between auditors and auditees in terms of their quality perceptions of the internal audit product. This expectation gap may have serious consequences for any internal audit service faced with the challenge of competition either externally or through an internal market. The existence of this expectations gap is a question for management and in particular audit management.

Carcello (1992) contended that an important factor in audit quality was

Table 8

Auditee Managers Compared to Auditor Managers

Key Word	t-value
Show a True and Fair Position	4.8
Error finding	4.4
Detecting	3.8
Checking	3.6
Expertise	3.5
Ticking	3.4
Specialist Skills	3.3
Ensure Legality	3.2
Prevent Fraud	2.9
Inspecting	2.5

seen to be a responsiveness to client needs. This line of thought was also considered by Sawyer (1990) who argued that, to be successful, an audit manager required the same qualities of leadership as a successful business manager. For the audit manager, this required an empathy with the auditee.

Strategy for the Future
From the empirical evidence, it seems legitimate to suggest that a new audit philosophy is required which will create an appropriate organisational environment within which a quality-driven, customer-orientated service can be effectively delivered. Several writers have supported this view. Peters (1992) discussing "The Quality Revolution" suggests the need for a continuous improvement in the performance of all processes in an organisation where audit itself should be seen as a quality system. This

should lead, Peters argues, to greater effectiveness and long-term competitive advantages. Grossi (1992) considers that internal auditors must have a fundamental grasp of managing quality by developing a realistic perspective of the internal audit's product and clients and by doing so help to shape the future role of the auditor – a proactive approach.

Getting closer to the customer is not without its risks. Carnell (1993) argues that although it is claimed that quality is enhanced by competition, which will turn audit into a quasi-business unit, bidding each year for its custom, the danger is that the pace of change is so great that audit's scope for planning its own work has been crowded out. The consequences of this crowding out is that if audit's end product is client-driven and quality is what the client makes it, audit may be on course to self-destruct.

Conclusion
It seems reasonable to conclude that it is a fusion of the positive perceptions of both the purchaser and provider of audit services that will itself define the meaning of quality audit services. The key areas for a perceptual consensus are shown in Table 9.

Table 9
A Strategy for the Future
A) Current Perceptual Agreement exists on the following:

1. PROFESSIONALISM
2. SERVICE TO MANAGEMENT
3. OBJECTIVITY

B) Audit Managers rate highly:

1. REPORTING
2. RECOMMENDING IMPROVEMENTS
3. INNOVATION

C) Auditee Managers rate highly:

1. ACHIEVE VALUE FOR MONEY
2. ANALYTICAL
3. ACHIEVE IMPROVEMENTS IN QUALITY

It may be contended that the way forward for internal audit is to promote all of the currently agreed high-quality perceptions of internal auditing (Section A above). They should then demonstrate to their "customers" that they can and are willing to deliver those services and skills highly rated by auditee management (Section C above) and that the means of doing this is through the positive auditing characteristics of recommending improvements through innovation and that the most appropriate vehicle for achieving this is the audit report. This is not to say that there can never be any reference to the regularity role of the auditor who must at some time come into contact with issues of legality, fraud and errors.

However it is now clear that any probity or like issues must be discussed with clients in direct connection with those highly-rated qualities given in section C above. For example, the potential for a major fraud could be explained in terms of a complete lack of quality or value-for-money rather than focusing on the probity issues directly.

Whichever way forward each individual audit manager decides is appropriate, it is obvious that as every contact between an auditor and an auditee conveys a quality impression of the audit process to the auditee then a start can be made immediately in not bridging but dissolving the quality expectations gap. The next contact may be the vital one.

The authors of this chapter have agreed in conjunction with the Audit Panel of the Chartered Institute of Public Finance and Accountancy to carry out a new survey within the public sector on quality issues affecting internal audit. This major survey will examine quality issues as reflected in current auditing guidelines and will try to show the impact of those guidelines on auditors and auditees alike. The new research will extend the database created by the previous research and should provide the opportunity to create a unique database showing "norms" or indicators of what acceptable levels of quality auditing provision are taken to be.

By increasing their awareness of the quality issues involved on both a national and local basis the providers should be able to increase their chances of success in the marketplace both in the range of audit services possible and the percentage of these that are taken up by the purchaser. Hopefully this chapter will stimulate some debate on the issues raised or the way forward for future research.

Appendix 1: Key words used in the Questionnaire:

Objectives	Activities	Qualities/Skills
Achieve V.F.M	Advising	
Achieve improvements in quality	Appraising	Analytical
Add value to the organisation's service provision	Checking	Computer literacy
Ensure compliace with regulations	Consulting	Confidence
Ensure legality	Criticising	Efficiency
Maintain standards	Detecting	Expertise
Maintain accountability	Error finding	Independence
Obtain assurance	Evaluating	Innovative
Aid planning	Gather evidence	Objectivity
Prevent fraud		Professionalism
Protect assets	Guiding	Qualifications
Recommend improvements	Inspecting	Reliability
Show a true and fair position	Interviewing	Resourcefulness
	Investigating	Sense of responsibility
	Monitoring	
	Observing	Specialist skills
	Questioning	Technical skills
	Reporting	
	Service to Management	
	Testing	
	Ticking	

References

Atchley, K. (1993) "Marketing Practice far from Perfect" *Financial Times* November

APC (Auditing Practices Committee) (1990) *Guidance for internal auditors, Guideline 308 Objectives and Scope of Internal Audit* APC

Carcello, J. V., Hermanson. R. H., McGrath, N. T. (1992) "Audit Quality Attributes: The Perceptions of Audit Partners, Preparers, and Financial Statement Users" *Auditing: A Journal of Practice and Theory* Vol 11 Iss 1, Spring pp1–15

Carnell, R. (1993) "Holy Grail or Poisoned Chalice?" *Management Accounting* Vol 71 Iss 3 March pp34–44

Chartered Institute of Public Finance and Accountancy *Quality – Internal Auditor* CIPFA

Gibbs, J. (1993) "Internal Auditing's Role in Quality Initiatives" *Internal Auditor* Vol 50 Iss 2 April p63

Grossi, G. (1992) "Quality Certifications" *Internal Auditor* Vol 49. Iss 5 October pp33–35

Hogan, W. M. (1994) "How to apply T.Q.M to the Internal Audit Function" *Internal Auditing* Vol 9 Iss 3 Winter pp3–14

Humphrey, C. M., Mozier, P., Turley, S. (1992) "The Audit Expectations Gap in Britain: An Empirical Investigation" *Accounting and Business Research* Vol 23 Iss 91A pp 395–411

Johnson, H. J. (1992) "The Internal Audit Widget" *Internal Auditor* Vol 49 Iss 2 April pp46–47

Morgan, G. and Pattinson, B. (1975) *The Role and Objectives of an Internal Audit – A Behavioural Approach* CIPFA

Peters, B. J. (1992) "The Quality Revolution" *Internal Auditor* Vol 49 Iss 2 April pp20–24

Powell S. F. (1993) "Internal Audit in Industry" *Management Accounting* Vol 71 Iss 8 September pp52–54

Sawyer, L. B. (1990) "The Leadership side of Internal Auditing" *Internal Auditor* Vol 47 Iss 4 August pp16–24

5

Accounting for the Environment

Brendan Quirke

Introduction

In the late 1980s, environmental concerns that had long remained dormant quite suddenly came to the forefront of public opinion. Concerns over the impact of the "greenhouse" effect, destruction of the rainforests, acid rain, increasingly high levels of pollution and depletion of natural resources received wide publicity. Companies initially responded defensively, to deflect the attentions of green pressure groups and of course to comply with the law. However, opportunities were also presented by the advent of the green consumer who was willing to pay a premium for products that were perceived as being "environmentally friendly", however dubious the reality. Green investment also began to become more prominent. As companies became "greener", it was inevitable that the accounting profession would have to consider its response to the emerging green agenda. As Owen (1993) observes, such developments would have considerable repercussions for accounting, particularly if companies used their annual reports as the major means of communication in respect of environmental and social issues; this would require "green" management information systems in support.

In formulating a response to the challenges presented by attempting to "green" the accounting function there are difficult issues to address. Hines (1991) makes the point that nature is excluded from accounting. Natural resources are interdependent, rain forests cannot be separated from soil. Rain forests help to absorb carbon dioxide, the trees prevent soil erosion.

But as Hines (1991) states, accounting names and separates. How can accounting quantify fresh air or a sunset? Therefore, at present, accounting methodology is fundamentally flawed when it comes to recognising environmental and economic interdependence.

There are two principal reasons for this condition. Firstly, accountants cannot account for the full costs of production, including the costs of consuming essential natural resources, such as air, water and land, because these resources have no assigned monetary value. Accountants are trained to measure financial transactions rather than the consumption of resources. Secondly, accounting rules and conventions penalise rather than encourage environmentally-aware companies. As Maunders and Burritt (1991 p11) point out there is a "mis-match between accounting information and its application to ecological issues". Ceteris paribus, the more a company spends on prevention and clean-up, the more downward pressure on its earnings per share, the magic number. As Rubenstein (1991) has said, we lack a vehicle for recording "green assets" and monitoring their use, for distinguishing between the costs of renewable versus non-renewable resources and for providing accounting incentives to improve environmental protection. Although one must also bear in mind that companies who can exhibit their "green" credentials can reap commercial success, for example Body Shop. This area of debate gives rise to a number of issues:

1. Accountability – To whom is the organisation accountable? To the investor alone, or to the wider community and future generations?
2. Externalities – An activity by one agent can cause a loss of welfare to another agent; this loss of welfare is uncompensated. Can the polluter be made to pay?
3. Missing markets and prices – Markets do not exist for certain inputs into and outputs from the productive process, for example fresh air and seawater, nor for certain outputs such as dirty water, dirty air and reduced raw materials. Can prices be arrived at, that is "shadow prices", which are non-market observed prices, to be used in lieu of existing market prices, or where market prices do not exist. Can these be introduced into the costing methodology?

These issues, together with some potential solutions to the problems identified, are discussed below. This chapter examines the above issues; considers how the loss of welfare associated with pollution can be compensated; discusses the changes to present accounting practice that there would need to be to reflect the environmental impact of organisational activity, such as new internal accounting systems and external reporting requirements. Finally, the chapter considers whether the concept of leasing our use of the environment from future generations would help to promote inter-generational equity.

Accountability

Accountability, as Perks (1993 p24) points out, simply means the obligation to give an account: "To clarify what is meant by accountability in a particular situation we should ask (1) *who* is accountable (2) *to whom*, (3) *how* (by what means) and (4) *for what*?" At present, companies are accountable principally to investors. People who buy shares are deemed to have a prior set of rights where disclosure is concerned, as opposed to the community at large. One can describe this relationship in terms of "agency theory".The parties involved in a particular accountability relationship can be referred to as principal (the accountee, for example shareholders) and the Agent (the accountor, for example directors). As Perks (1993) states, principals pass control of their resources to the agents on the basis of a contractual relationship that requires information to be provided; this is governed by legislation. Much more is implied by this relationship: shareholders expect that good care will be taken of their money, but also that the company will be profitable and also efficient and effective. The accounting model of accountability is based on the notion that the owners or shareholders are distinct from the managers and directors and that there is a need for directors to be accountable to shareholders. However, as has been mentioned above, this is just one view of accountability. Perks (1993) also points out that there is a wider view that can be taken.

The case for a wider view of accountability has been put forward by the Corporate Report which was published in 1975. All significant economic entities were seen as having an implicit duty to report publicly whether or not this was required by law or regulation. As Perks (p36) points out "they saw public accountability as being in addition to legal obligations and argued that it arises from the custodial role played in the community by economic entities". The Corporate Report identified various user groups in society ranging from the equity investment group through to government and of course the public and thus played an important part in expanding the involvement of the accounting function in the accountability of organisations to different groups in society.

There is, however, much debate about the nature and impact of greater accountability inside and outside the accounting profession. In the 1970s, there were, as Perks (1993) states, pressures to widen accountability: more and more organisations were expected to be accountable to an increasing number of interest groups and indeed to society as a whole. In the 1980s there were calls for greater accountability. Central government saw itself as representing the public interest and organisations in the public service sector such as local authorities, health authorities and so on were expected to be publicly accountable for the resources that they used. Those who call for increased accountability usually see themselves as being the principals, and they expect that those who they consider to be their agents should be made more accountable to them. Therefore, principals are calling for more power over agents. There is an implication here, according to Perks, that accountability is a subjugating force; that it tends to reduce the freedom of those who can be controlled by principals. Gray (1992) sees accountability as emancipatory in that it exposes, enhances and develops social relationships through a re-examination and expansion of established rights to information.

Similarly, Power (1991) states that the most general model of accountability is that of principal and agent. He believes that the analytical problem is to construct forms of "contract" which will provide the agent with incentives to act in the principal's interests. He goes on to state that under certain very specific modelling conditions it will be in the agent's own self-interest to submit to particular and costly contractual arrangements which make his or her actions visible to the principal. "In general the principal requires both that the agent act towards a particular end and that these actions are rendered visible by some form of account(ing)" Power (p32). Auditing could be said to be relevant here as a form of monitoring which enhances the credibility of the flow of information from the agent to the principal.

Power (1991) questions the neutrality of accounting and auditing by deconstructing the assumptions underlying the general accountability model. For example, in pollution control, society may be regarded as the principal and the polluter whose actions cannot be fully monitored as the agent. He questions the identity of the principal. "Who or what is society? What are its aims, aspirations and interests ... Thus one problem in articulating environmental accountability is the very characterisation of the principal itself, i.e. who it is to whom agents are accountable" (p34).

Power also suggests that when accountability is narrowly premised upon contracting arrangements, the essentially contestable social conditions which make possible contracting or bonding processes between principal and agent are not in view. He asks the questions: "What is the nature of the action of the agent which is relevant to the postulated relations of accountability? What are the environmentally significant performances of the business entity and in what forms of expertise are such judgements of significance to be expressed"(p35). Power suggests the possibility of selectivity and bias in the technical possibility of knowing the environmental effects of certain corporate actions. Certainly, Roberts and Scapens (1985 p454) recognise that the "image of organisations given in accounts is a partial, selective and potentially distorted reflection of the flow of events and procedures that constitute organisational life". It is analogous to an image rather than a snapshot of a particular organisation at a particular point in time.

That being the case, Roberts and Scapens go on to state (p450) that "real power of accounting lies in the way in which as a structure of meaning, it comes to define what shall and shall not count as significant within an organisation". This does bring into question the neutrality and objectivity of accounting. Power also acknowledges the difficulties concerning the role of accounting within recent environmental initiatives. He believes that there is an important tension "between a role for traditional accounting practices and knowledge, where notions of audit, systems and budget are all essential elements in the greening of organisations, and the risk of overvaluing our ability to attach financial numbers to things and events" (p36). Thus there is an important issue here concerning the nature and mix of the expertise to be incorporated into the environmental audit process and the role of accounting-based techniques and knowledge. There is a view of accounting as part of the problem rather than the solution and Power (1992) quotes Gorz, who believes the calculative rationality contained within accounting practices needs to be rejected to ensure an authentic relationship with nature. Power (p36) quotes Douglas and Wildavsky to express the fear that if environmental audit is dependent upon accounting-based standards of performance, then it may "tend to give undue prominence to values that can be calculated, not necessarily to the most significant". Therefore when commentators like Dewar (1991) call for better public accountability and full information disclosure which can be independently scrutinised and investigated, that is audited, the notion of environmental accountability is not uncontested.

Power (1991) believes that we need not be committed to a formalised interpretation of the accountability structure and that auditing may actually go so far to construct relations of accountability. "Indeed, audit may create or distort both the self-consciousness of principals as principals and the criteria of relevance for the visibility of corporate action" (p37). Thus the concept of environmental audit is something that is according to Power

(1991) "negotiable". There is a spectrum of possibilities that could in his words (p37) span protest and professionalisation.

Protest could be said to require corporate entities to explain and justify their actions to a wider audience; the monitoring of information that already exists lies in the professionalisation end of the spectrum. Power (1991) quotes Armstrong (1991) in arguing that audit is bound up with strategies of passification and routinisation using the disinterested language of expertise which should generate neutral representation. Certainly the environmental audit services that are used by corporate actors and indeed offered by accountancy firms do seem to emphasise the management control and compliance aspects of environmental auditing. The International Chamber of Commerce certainly speaks in these terms, in its position paper on Environmental Auditing. There is concern therefore that environmental audit may well be constrained towards the professionalisation rather than the protest end of this particular spectrum.

Gray (1992) believes that the development of accountability should increase the transparency of organisations. It should increase the number of things that are made visible as well as increase the number of ways in which things are made visible and so encourage increasing openness. In order to achieve greater openness it would seem necessary to resort to law to determine the type of audit that would be undertaken as environmental audit can range from a simple compliance report to an overall evaluation of environmental management systems and organisational interactions with the environment. Also, there would appear to be a need for legal obligation for full public disclosure of the environmental audit report. It might also be possible to establish the office of Auditor General for the Environment to oversee the whole process. From the above discussion it seems certain that this process will not be without difficulties but a start needs to be made.

Externalities
As stated above, an external cost exists when two conditions prevail: an activity by one agent causes a loss of welfare to another agent; and the loss of welfare is uncompensated. According to economic theory, a socially-optimal level of economic activity does not coincide with the private optimum if external costs are present. How can the social optimum be reached? This begs the question of government intervention. Pollution is an externality; how can the person suffering from pollution be compensated? In other words how can that externality be internalised. One way of attempting to do this would be by the construction of an environmental lease. This will be considered below.

Missing Markets and Prices

One of the major challenges facing the accountant in attempting to account for the impact of organisations upon the environment is that no prices exist for certain inputs into and outputs from the productive process. As accountants can only measure things which have a price tag or monetary value upon them, the absence of prices is a major handicap.

The reason there are no market prices is there are no markets for these particular inputs into and outputs from the productive process. To overcome this obstacle, "shadow prices" could be introduced. As Quirke (1991) says, a "shadow price" is a non-market observed price. Shadow pricing attempts to place a price tag on resources which, once achieved, allows the relative scarcity of a resource to be measured. Once price tags have been put on resources, accountants will be able more completely to match costs with revenues.

A number of approaches can be used to determine shadow prices. One very direct approach is to ask people questions, such as: "What price would you put on clean air?" In this sense, a shadow price can be anything people are willing to pay. Another approach, identified by Cairncross (1991), is that economists hunt for a real world market in which to try to capture the value of environmental assets. For example, two identical houses within the same geographical area may sell for differing amounts. One is next to a factory (the cheaper one) and the other is some distance away. The price difference could be the value that people place on peace and quiet and lack of pollution. The problem here is that it would be a local shadow price specific to a designated area and not capable of more general application.

Another kind of shadow price identified by Cairncross (1991) may be reflected in what people pay to visit a particular forest or park. The assumption is that, even if visiting the forest is free, the cost of travelling there gives some idea of the value that people put on it. This is known as the travel cost method, (TCM). As Milne (1991) observes, the travel cost method is straightforward in principle, but suffers from a number of disadvantages. The travel cost method includes the total of vehicle-related costs and opportunity costs of on-site and travel time. The difficulties inherent in estimating the value of time have not yet been attended to according to Pearce and Markandya (1989).

Environmental damage can have measurable costs. When air pollution corrodes stone, the cost of repairs can be calculated and this is a means by which the value of cleaner air may be estimated. The cost of cleaning up the ocean after an oil spillage could be calculated, and thus the value of cleaner seawater could be derived. The price of fresh air could be set at the same price as the filtration equipment which purifies air before it is returned to the atmosphere. There is an element of subjectivity in the above approaches, and it is recognised that there could be a wide disparity in prices, but they do at least represent a start.

Gray (1992) calls for a shadow accounting system that could produce numbers "which can be deducted from calculated accounting profit and be expended in the restoration of the biosphere"(p419). It seems feasible to suggest that such an accounting system would have to make use of shadow prices in order to produce such "numbers".

What Role for Accountants
Given the nature of the subject, it is perhaps predictably the case that agreement does not exist amongst accounting academics as to the role of accounting in relation to the environment. Cooper (1992 p16) actually questions whether accounting has any positive role to play in this respect. She states "We have lived for too long with accounting's treatment of so-called externalities . . . a treatment resulting in . . . nature . . . being trampled over and discarded in the search for profits . . .". and believes that certain initiatives are actually more damaging than helpful, for example, the distinction between man-made and natural capital.

Man-made capital as Gray et al (1993) state includes those elements from the biosphere that are no longer part of the harmony of the natural ecology. This includes machines, buildings, roads and so on. Natural capital includes those elements of the biosphere that are essential for life and which, for the purposes of sustainability, as Gray et al identify, must remain inviolate, such as the ozone layer, as well as those elements which are renewable, such as woodlands, or for which reasonable substitutes can be found, such as energy from fossil fuels. Cooper believes this distinction to be false. In her opinion it could lead to a situation where the natural environment and its sustainability are placed ahead of the lives and living conditions of human beings. Cooper (1992 p26) sees accounting as a system of "binary opposites". If we try to account for nature then in her view we are forcing the multiplicity of nature into the binary opposites of accounting which is "violence against nature". She sees the profit motive as leading to the destruction of the environment and that if we try to account for nature even more profits will be squeezed from nature because of the obsession with the bottom line.

Power (1992) sees green accounting as an empty canvas. He is concerned that accountants may capture environmental issues and professionalise and proceduralise them. Therefore there is perhaps a need for a new accounting, though he does not go on to specify what that new accounting should be. He believes the problem of valuing the environment is controversial and the question of monetarisation is indeed central to this. Is money a "convenient measuring rod"? The intention of environmental economists like Pearce for example, is to emphasise that the environment is not a "free good"; this must lead to consideration of prices. The concerns expressed by both Cooper and Power are recognised in Gray, Walters, Bebbington and Thompson (1995 p214) but they see more optimistically perhaps that "environmental accounting can represent new voices, new visibilities and new discourses which can disrupt and encourage possibilities for change". There may well be a need for a new accounting, but there is a role for accounting to play.

Gray (1990) puts forward a number of ideas on how internal accounting and reporting systems might look. He suggests environmental budgets where levels of environmental activity could be allocated to activity centres and elements of reward and penalty systems could be tied to the satisfaction of allocated budget levels. Gray also calls for environmental impact assessment of new projects and the introduction of hurdle rates which would act as a filtering mechanism to ensure that all new investment meets environmental criteria. In environmental terms, the hurdle rate would be the cost of environmental capital, just as in conventional investment appraisal the cut off rate must equal the cost of conventional capital. What the cost of environmental capital will be, still has to be determined. Much work still needs to be done.

Gray suggests the need for environmental asset accounting and maintenance. He believes that ownership involves stewardship – the responsibility to care for and maintain assets on behalf of the human race, other forms of life and future generations. The organisation should categorise environmental assets under its ownership and those under its control. To account for them, Gray argues for part of natural capital to be regarded as intangible assets. There should be monitoring of the maintenance, enhancement and depletion of natural capital, as well as auditing transfers between natural capital and man-made capital.

External Reporting

With regard to external reporting, Gray (1990) considers that reporting could consist of an environmental policy statement, an environmental expenditure statement, an emission statement, disclosure of natural and man-made assets and transfers between asset categories. This would lead to greater disclosure and increased transparency.

Disclosure of natural and man-made assets is particularly important. There is as Gray (1990) recognises, an urgent need to distinguish man-made from natural capital. There is a further need to distinguish critical capital from other natural capital. For example, in biodiversity, resources such as the ozone layer are non-renewable and should not be diminished in any way. Equity demands that we pass the same value of natural capital from this generation to the next generation. The equity concept will not be observed unless we try to value in some way the stock of natural capital and consider to what extent it is diminished in the production of man-made capital, as well as the substitution rate between the two types of capital.

There is important work to be done in trying to categorise assets. A possible starting point is to recognise, as Gray (1990) does, that an important part of natural capital will be intangible, initially because prices do not exist. He calls for transfers between categories of asset to be tracked and to be disclosed in financial reports. Shadow pricing will play a crucial role here, because it will enable values to be computed and to appear in financial statements, where they can be subject to audit scrutiny.

Leasing

The philosophy underpinning environmental economics and accounting is that we hold the environment in trust for future generations. If this is the case, then we could make some sort of payment to them for use of the environment and the consequences that such use implies. One means by which we may be able to achieve this goal is by taking out a lease upon the environment. However, this raises a number of questions, such as the precise meaning of the term "lease", which elements would make up a lease payment for use of the environment, who would be the lessor, and who would be the lessee? The rest of this section considers these issues in addition to problems associated with natural capital.

Definitions

A lease is a method or contract by which a company or organisation acquires the use of an asset for a period of time in exchange for the payment of rent. The practice of leasing is a means by which a company can gain the use of an asset without the payment of rent and without investing a capital sum.

There are two types of lease. The first of these is an operating lease, which generally has a short duration and the equipment leased is often used for less than its full economic life. The lessee does not bear the full economic cost of the asset becoming obsolete or inoperational. The second form of lease is a finance (or capital) lease, taken on a large item over a long period. The lessor buys the asset and is the legal owner, but the lessee company uses the asset in its business in return for paying a rental or hire charge to the lessor.

In considering which type of lease would be more appropriate in the use of the environment, a capital lease would appear the more suitable. The reasons for this are firstly, that such a lease would have to be taken out over a long period of time, say 99 years, and secondly, that the legal (or at least moral) owners of the environment are future generations - the lessee could be said to be using the environment in pursuit of business, so a parallel could be drawn with the more common type of capital lease.

Lessor and Lessee

If leasing is to be considered a viable option in the field of environmental accounting, a basic question that must be answered is, "Who is to be the lessor and who is to be the lessee?" We lease the environment from future generations, so surely we must be cast in the position of the lessee. This much is reasonably straightforward. However, it is more complex to decide who is going to be the lessor. We lease the environment from future generations, so surely they must be the lessor. This is certainly logical, but it is hardly practical. Future generations, by definition, are not in a position to oversee the operation of the lease. The only feasible solution is for the government to act as an agent or proxy for future generations.

Environmental Leasing

In trying to derive the components of an environmental lease, one must consider exactly what is taking place when resources are being consumed. It is a reasonable assumption that if resources are being consumed capital stock in terms of natural resources is being depleted. Natural resources include the stock of fresh air, fresh water, etc. Accordingly, the first part of the lease term should include an element for the depleted value of natural capital. There is also a risk to future generations of depleted resources and a polluted environment, so the second element of the lease should include a payment to future generations for the risk involved. A third element of the lease should be a return for the use of natural capital. This a reasonable proposal: providers of man-made capital expect a return on their investment and it is no less equitable for the providers of natural capital, in this case future generations, to receive such a return. Government would act as their proxy. The lease payment should therefore comprise the following constituent parts:

$$L = cK + I + K\,(1\text{-}c)r$$

where cK is the depleted value of natural capital; where I is the insurance premium paid to future generations for the risk of depleting natural capital; and where K (1-c)r is the return for the use of natural capital.

Natural Capital

In order to assess the depleted value of natural capital, it makes sense to define exactly what we mean by the term natural capital. Common (1988) defines natural resources as all those things "available to man as gifts of nature". All of the links between economic activity and the natural environment involve the use of natural resources. They are exploited by man as sources of food, raw materials and energy.

Common further states that natural resources exist in the environment as stocks from which economic activity draws flows of input. The major distinction drawn in economic analysis is between living and non-living stocks, with the former known as renewable and the latter as non-renewable natural resources. Renewable resources, by definition, reproduce over time, while non-renewable resources do not. Animal and plant populations are classed as renewable resources; mineral deposits are classed as non-renewable. Natural capital also includes, amongst others, tropical forests, ocean habitats, wetlands and fisheries, atmospheres and stratospheres.

Depletion of Natural Capital

As non-renewable resources are exploited and more pollutants are released into the atmosphere, the value of natural capital must be diminished. For those elements of natural capital which do not have a market price, a shadow price will have to be calculated. This will enable each element of natural capital to be built into the lease payment so that the lease can fully reflect the impact upon the environment.

Insurance Premium for Future Generations

There is a risk to future generations that natural capital will be exhausted or severely depleted by preceding generations. Within the concept of inter-generational equity, a payment should be made to them to cover the risk of this happening. This is the second element of the lease payment.

This concept has already been applied to some degree in Canada and the United States. Hartwick and Oleweiler (1986) outline the workings of the Alberta Heritage Savings Fund and the Alaskan Permanent Fund. Resource royalties are paid into the funds, which are then invested, and the principal and interest will be available to future generations. The accumulated principal represents a stock of wealth above ground in the place of part or all of the depleted resource stock below ground.

The problem for government will be deciding upon which investment strategy to follow: whether to invest in industrial expansion or in the securities and bonds markets. This will depend on the contingencies in existence at any point in time. The percentage figure of royalties which should form the basis of the premium to future generations is very difficult to estimate. Royalties in the range of 10 to 15 percent are considered to be a realistic reflection of the risk to future generations of resources becoming depleted, but whether this would be politically acceptable is another matter. One must bear in mind that future generations cannot yet vote.

Return for the Use of Natural Capital

In the conventional financial world, providers of long-term funds expect a return for their investment. A company pays back principal plus interest. There is no reason why this principle should not apply in environmental accounting. The final component of the lease payment therefore takes note of this concept.

Companies and organisations are using natural capital as an input into their productive process and as a "repository" in which to discharge or emit outflows from that process. As natural capital is assumed to be provided by future generations, then the return which they receive should be in the range of the company's weighted average cost of capital which is the minimum return required by the providers of long-term funds.

Conclusions

There is as yet no consensus about the role for accounting in trying to account for the environment. The issues explored above such as account-ability, externalities and shadow pricing would be seen by some observers as attempts to capture environmental issues, neutralise them and indeed make them safe for accounting and accountants. There would be some commen-tators who see no benefit if accounting becomes involved in environmental issues. These charges as Gray et al (1995) recognise will have to be addressed. The concept of an environmental lease is put forward as one step along the path to a more complete accounting. It might be anathema to some, it may well offer food for thought to others. Surely, something has to be done.

References

Cairncross, F. (1991) *Costing the Earth* The Economist Books Ltd

Common, M. (1988) *Environment and Resource Economics: An Introduction* Longman

Cooper, C. (1992) "The Non and Nom of Accounting for (M)other Nature" *Accounting, Auditing & Accountability* Vol 5 No3 pp16–39

Dewar, D. (1991) "Accountability with a capital 'E' " *Public Finance and Accountancy* 12 July pp8–9

Gray, R.H. (1990) *The Greening of Accountancy: The profession after Pearce* Certified Accountants Publications Ltd London

Gray, R.H. (1992) "Accounting and environmentalism: an exploration of the challenge of gently accounting for accountability, transparency and sustainability" *Accounting, Organisations and Society* Vol 17 No 5 pp399–426

Gray, R.H., Bebbington, J. and Walters, D. (1993) *Accounting For The Environment* PCP

Gray, R.H., Walters, D., Bebbington, J. and Thompson, I. (1995) "The Greening of Enterprise: An Exploration of the (Non) Role of Environmental Accounting and Environmental Accountants in Organisational Change" *Critical Perspectives on Accounting* Vol 6 pp211–239

Hartwick, J.M. and Oleweiler, N.D. (1986) *The Economics of Natural Resource Use* Harper and Row New York

Hines, R. (1991) "On Valuing Nature" *Accounting, Auditing & Accountability* Vol 4, No 3, pp27–29

Maunders, K.T. (1991) "Accounting and Ecological Crisis" *Accounting, Auditing & Accountability* Vol 4, No 3 pp9–26

Milne, M.J. (1991) "Accounting, Environmental Resource Values, and Non-market Valuation Techniques: A Review" *Accounting Auditing & Accountability* Vol 4 No 3 pp81–109

Owen, D. (1993) "The Emerging Green Agenda" In D. Smith (ed) *Business and the Environment* pp55–74

Pearce, D.W. Markandya, A. and Barbier, E.B. (1989) *Blueprint for a Green Economy* London Earthscan

Pearce, D.W. and Turner, R.K. (1990) *Economics of Natural Resources and the Environment* Harvester Wheatsheaf.

Perks, R.W. (1993) *Accounting and Society* Chapman and Hall

Power, M. (1991) "Auditing and Environmental Expertise: Between protest and professionalism" *Accounting, Auditing & Accountability* Vol 4 No 3 pp30–42

Power, M. (1992) "After calculation? Reflections on Critique of Economic

Reason by Andre Gorz" *Accounting, Organisations and Society* Vol 17 No 5 pp477–500

Quirke, B.J. (1991) *Accounting for the Environment: Current Issues. European Environment* Vol 1 Part 5 October 1991 pp19–22

Roberts, J. and Scapens, R. (1985) "Accounting Systems and Systems of Accountability" *Accounting, Organisations and Society* Vol 10 No4 pp443–56

Rubenstein, D. (1991) "Lessons of Love" *CA Magazine (Canada)* March

6

Public Sector Audit: the First and Last Defence against Fraud?

Alan Doig

Introduction

Power has rested with Conservative governments since 1979. Amid the current concern over standards in public life (Wilson and Doig 1995) two questions have emerged: what is the likely organisational and cultural impact of the changes wrought to both public and private sectors and with whom should lie the responsibility for policing some of the less welcome consequences of the changes?

While some of the effects of the comprehensive and continuing change that governments have introduced to both public and private sectors are only now being realised, it would appear that the faith in the efficacy of unfettered market forces has, on the one hand, led to the promotion of entrepreneurial activity, the removal of controls from commercial and financial sectors, the encouragement of financial gain as a reward for and an indicator of worth and hard work, and the transformation in the organisation, development and delivery of products and services. On the other hand, while the integration of both corporate and individual aspirations has been achieved through combining company profit margins with management commissions, bonuses, performance-related pay, and share options, the accumulation of wealth, the display of material success, and the promotion of personal ambition has also left a downside of greed, acquisitiveness and pursuit of individual ambition which has seen both employees and management prepared to use corporate resources and personal position to cut corners to achieve status and growth. In his 1988 Hibbert Lecture on BBC Radio 4, a City solicitor had warned that "with licensed greed creeps in the dry rot of corruption. For the value-system which tolerates the one will not be likely to resist the other, if that is necessary to achieve 'success' " (*The Listener* 1988).

Three years later the headlines appeared to reinforce the message. In 1991 the Roger Levitt Group collapsed with losses of £40 million; Levitt was subsequently charged and convicted. Polly Peck administrators accused its founder, Asil Nadir, of perpetrating the biggest fraud in English commercial history as, allegedly, some £550 million was redirected out of the company into a byzantine network of offshore companies. Nearly a thousand Lloyd names made history as they attempted to sue an underwriter; their counsel told the judge that never in the commercial history of the City of London had so much of other people's money been lost by the single-handed negligence of one man. The Bank of England closed down the Bank of Credit and Commerce International; one of its employees said that the bank would bribe God. Robert Maxwell fell off his luxury motor cruiser and debts of £3 billion, looted from his pension funds to sustain his business activities, were quickly discovered. (*Sunday Times* 1991) The Serious Fraud Office announced that the sum lost through white-collar fraud in 1991 was double that lost in household burglaries; the main victims have often been small investors and pensioners.

Moreover, many of the cases were perpetrated internally, and often by a senior level of management who had evinced no earlier propensity toward criminal conduct. Deregulation, encouragement of an enterprise culture and lax supervision appeared to have led to a significant shift in behaviour that had implications for the overall integrity of the sector.

> [I]f wrongdoings . . . mount beyond a certain level, many within the fields affected will become cynical, encouraged to sharp practice themselves to compete, and unwilling to give evidence against wrongdoers, still less blow the whistle. Only in an environment where high standards prevail will practitioners feel the sense of indignation and personal security essential to denounce the wrongdoer promptly and accurately. In turn, high ethical standards cannot be encouraged except by measures to ensure competence, disclosure of dealings, and inspections to enforce compliance with public standards and procedures (Clarke 1986 p186).

For the private sector, the responsibility of external audit for both the prevention and detection of wrongdoing is still, this chapter suggests, a subject for debate. On the other hand, public sector external audit has had the means to detect and report on the dysfunctional consequences of change during the 1980s. Not only could the one sector learn from the other but external audit in both sectors could be the first and last defence against fraud, waste and mismanagement.

Barlow Clowes and BCCI – Should the Buck Stop with (and Be Paid For by) the External Auditor?

Precisely which external agency should implement and police such measures has been the subject of concern during the 1980s. Fraud has never been particularly high on the list of police priorities, which are determined by the political agenda where public order and crimes against the person and property predominate. The police's difficulty with the investigation of fraud is in part the public perception and in part the nature of the crime:

> . . . public order is not violated in business offences as it is in conventional crime. There is normally no violence to persons or property, and the conduct in question takes place in private not public places, between people with a pre-existing and usually continuing relationship . . . its privacy and complexity makes it difficult to investigate; the pre-existing relationships between victim and offender make for the likelihood of claim and counter-claim as to who occupies which role; and in many cases the police may take the view that their victims have only themselves to blame for their lack of caution, or have the necessary resources to remedy the situation by civil action (Clarke 1990 p22).

At the same time companies may be reluctant to invoke criminal fraud investigations for fear of publicising the incidence of fraud, as well as seeking to protect their public reputation and the public's confidence in their activities, and in part a concern that a rigorous prosecutorial approach may damage customer service and may threaten market-share (Johnston 1992 pp106–7). Additionally, police intervention may be seen as disruptive to staff relationships and ongoing organisational functions as well as potentially embarrassing in terms of publicity and commercial credibility. Finally, fraud inquiries and trials are complex and costly. In the 1990 trial of those involved in the collapse of a Derbyshire theme park, for example, the inquiry involved: 402 witnesses interviewed; 531 statements; two courtrooms knocked into one to house the trial; each juror equipped with a computer screen for the 14000 pages of exhibits; 6 defendants; 27 charges of fraud, theft and obtaining money by deception. There were five convictions (with sentences from 4 years to a fine) and a cost to the Derbyshire police of £1.8 million (*Observer* (a) 1992).

Such considerations have important implications for resource allocation internally as well and also for those whose responsibility it is to deal with fraud.

> [T]he cuts in resources that the Metropolitan Police Company Fraud Department experienced in the 1980s forced them to prioritize cases more sharply on the basis of their *estimated* likelihood to yield a result. This may not have affected the numbers of recorded frauds or the clear-up rate but, *inter alia*, what the policy *has* done is to shift the economic burden of crime investigation onto victims, in particular corporate victims, and has thus transferred public law back into the sphere of private law (Levi 1987 p282).

This has essentially focused attention on regulatory and audit processes whose weaknesses have been highlighted by two cases: Barlow Clowes and BCCI. In its reform of the City, Conservative governments since 1979 have sought an expanding and deregulated financial sector but rather than seeking external policing backed by legislation (for example, a UK equivalent of the US Securities and Exchange Commission) the Conservative Government chose self-policing through the 1986 Financial Services Act. The responsibility for access, registration and regulation was devolved to a number of self-regulating bodies dealing with different parts of the sector, under the general authority of the Securities and Investment Board (SIB).

Until the 1986 Act took full effect, however, the Department of Trade and Industry (DTI) had a small office within its Financial Services Division that was responsible up to 1988 for licensing dealers. The Conservative Government's changes to the financial world inevitably put pressure on the unit to expedite the licencing of dealers even though, as in the case of Barlow Clowes and Partners, there was cause for concern. "I have no concrete reason to worry", wrote a DTI official, "although one naturally tends to look askance at business controlled from Gibraltar and harbour unworthy thoughts about the real motives in moving there." (Le Quesne 1988; Lever 1992).

Clowes's financial difficulties later persuaded the SIB to move against him. Unfortunately for them and the DTI, the receivers and the financial journalists managed to unearth some unflattering facts about Clowes with surprising ease and speed (Swiss and Jersey bank accounts, a large yacht, a vineyard, a network of over 50 companies, unsecured loans, and so on) while backbench MPs rushed to lead the increasing pressure from investors on the DTI to bail them out. The Le Quesne inquiry managed to show the DTI as fumbling and unintrusive and its ministers as the rubberstamps of their officials; both of which opened the way for MPs to demand that the Parliamentary Ombudsman investigate allegations of maladministration for failing to uncover the structure of the Clowes operation and financial position, and for continuing to licence Clowes.

This was duly proved, allowing the Government to pay compensation, something "decided at the highest level", without admitting liability, negligence or incompetence. While Clowes began a 10-year prison sentence in 1992 for his theft of some millions of pounds, so the Government, which had paid out over £150 million in compensation, began to look around for some means to claim that money back. Their target has been the company auditors, Spicer and Oppenheim (now part of Touche Ross). HM Treasury and Cork Gully, the liquidators, have issued writs in 1993 and, in 1995, a number of accountants from the firm were disciplined by the Institute of Chartered Accountants disciplinary committee for their professional conduct and the failure to take action on information which "if taken together, suggested that a possible fraud was being perpetrated by Mr Clowes in relation to the overseas client funds". What is increasingly at issue is the responsibility of the auditor for ensuring that the companies they audit are not indulging in fraudulent activity, and their financial responsibility for failing to spot such activity, which, since the BCCI case, also means that assurance must be timely.

BCCI was a Pakistan-founded bank (Adams and Frantz 1993) primarily intended to provide financial services to Muslims. Its rapid growth, its weak accounting procedures, its unorthodox lending practices, and its predilection for asking no questions of depositors made it popular with a variety of dirty-money practitioners from Panama's General Manuel Noriega to the CIA and the Abu Nidal terrorist group. Its loose internal controls also made it a target for its employees and favoured customers. After losses of nearly $500 million in 1989, and despite a last-minute attempt at rescue by the Abu Dhabi state in 1990, the BCCI was closed by the Bank of England on 5 July 1991. What emerged from the subsequent inquiries was that knowledge of the Bank's activities was available prior to the closure but that, up to the time Price Waterhouse had reported in March 1991 that the Bank had over $2 billion of bad or doubtful debts, there had been no means to identify or pursue the increasing signs of concern. In 1992, the Treasury and Civil Service Committee accepted the Bank of England's argument that "it is asking a lot of [auditors] or of supervisors necessarily to uncover deliberate and well designed fraud" and Price Waterhouse's argument that "even the best planned and executed audit will not necessarily discover a sophisticated fraud, especially one where there is collusion at the highest level of management and with third parties" (Treasury and Civil Service Committee 1991–2 para 37).

Nevertheless, Price Waterhouse is, too, the subject of writs, this time issued for $8billion against it and the second BCCI auditor, Ernst and Whinney (as it was at the time), by the bank's liquidators, Touche Ross. The incestuous exchange of writs between the various accountancy firms as plaintiffs for one case and defendants in another has increased substantially; since 1990, over 15 major claims are outstanding against major firms of accountants for negligence.

Management, Fraud and Audit: Cost and Cadbury
The concern over whose responsibility it is to prevent or detect fraud has led to a number of discussions among professional and representative bodies both about the function of audit and the wider issue of company governance and responsibility, both encouraged by the possible financial consequences of major litigation and the implications of unlimited liability under which most accountancy firm partners work (Gardiner 1995).

The issue of identifying fraud revolves around two issues: first, the role of auditors to conduct anti-fraud audits and, second, the distinction between the role of management and the role of the auditors. The private sector auditors argue that it is management's responsibility to draw up the accounts; it is the role of auditors to check them to state whether or not they represent a "true and fair view" of the company's position. The wider issue of management responsibility and accountability has been addressed by the Stock Exchange, the Financial Reporting Council and the accountancy profession which set up the Cadbury Committee. Its agenda concerned both board accountability and board responsibility in terms of the governance of the company: strategic aims, leadership, supervision of management and the stewardship of the company on behalf of shareholders. Its report (Cadbury 1992) included proposals to separate the roles of Chair and Chief Executive, the establishment of audit committees, directors' training, the role of internal audit, and the rotation of external auditors. While not wishing to make the reporting of suspicions of fraud a statutory requirement (the Bingham BCCI Report recommendation which the government accepted not only for banks but also for the rest of the regulated sector, such as building societies and investment business), it did see the need to ensure that external auditors reported such suspicions to the appropriate investigative authorities and proposed the use of audit committees as the route to air internal concerns with independent (and independent-minded) non-executive directors.

While some organisations, such as the Institute of Internal Auditors, have seen this as a way of raising the profile of internal audit (*Observer* (b) 1992) external auditors have been concerned over the absence of protection from actions for negligence or defamation and the time and costs involved. Said an Ernst and Young partner in 1993, "I do not think that management has any conception of how time-consuming and expensive it would be if auditors had to conduct all audits on the basis that all fraud, if it exists, should be detected" (*Independent* (a) 1993).

This has called into question and prompted a longrunning and still continuing debate on the role of the external auditor in relation to fraud and other financial misconduct. Critics of external auditors condemn them for the conflict of interest and sense of dependency in selling companies both audit services and other financial and advisory services which could not then be objectively audited by the same firm, for the poor quality of the annual audit and for the failure of the professional bodies to act against firms with demonstrably bad audit practices (*Observer* (c) 1992;*Observer* (d) 1992). Furthermore critics such as Labour MP Austin Mitchell point out that not only do external auditors not spot fraud but collude in the use of creative accountancy that provides the conditions of unaccountability and "grey zone" legality that promotes fraud (*Observer* (e) 1992, *Observer* (f) 1992; *Independent* (b) 1994). Yet his enthusiasm for an independent regulator, which may protect auditors from having to confront their paymasters over issues that might lose them the renewal of the contract, would go against the longstanding tradition of both the close relations between the company and the external auditor (*Independent* (c) 1994) and the hands-off policing by their professional bodies in overseeing the competence and objectivity of external auditors.

On the other hand, new standards issued in 1995 by the Auditing Practices Board now require auditors to assess the risk of material fraud and, in relation to the preparation of financial statements, give an opinion on whether material rule-breaking has taken place. Whether the search for material fraud or non-compliance and the wider issue of their integration with the role of audit committees may result in an improved role by both internal and external auditors in the prevention and detection of fraud in the private sector is still under discussion. Nevertheless, if they are encouraged to take a more proactive stance on fraud, then private sector external auditors will be coming from a very low base. In its 1988 survey of major commercial companies, Ernst and Young discovered that only 1% of fraud was uncovered by external auditors; by 1994 this was up to 2% (Ernst and Young 1995). It is not surprising that both the demand for a greater commitment from external audit in detecting fraud, and reforms to control dependency on clients, could look to the public sector experience where the external auditor has had much more success in tackling fraud and mismanagement and where, as the May 1995 decision of the National Audit Office to inform the World Health Organisation that it would not continue to audit its accounts when there was evidence of fraud demonstrated, the principled stance is possible under certain conditions (*Independent* (d) 1995).

Monitoring and Scrutiny: Audit and the Public Sector
The current roles and responsibilities of public sector external audit have derived from the increasing power of governments during the 1970s. It prompted those in Parliament with an interest in accountability and responsibility to seek to reform the various means of scrutiny and monitoring of the actions and activities of government. In 1978 the Committee on Procedure proposed a structured departmentally-based committee system that, with enough support of senior politicians on both sides, survived the defeat of the Labour Government in 1979 and was shepherded through the following year by Norman St. John-Stevas, the then Conservative Leader of the House. Although described as potentially "the most important parliamentary reforms of the century" the reforms were diluted and, while the new select committees undertook much worthy work, they carried out little effective scrutiny of or have had much influence on the activities of government. Suffering from inadequate resources, limitations of the scope of their investigations and their relevance to the decisionmaking processes, and ministerial disregard for their reports, their subsequent "scrutiny and investigative work . . . has, for the most part made little noticeable impact on government policy" (Adonis 1990 p108).

On the other hand, there was much more success in promoting legislation on behalf of a longstanding Commons committee, the Committee for Public Accounts (PAC), to secure the independence of the Exchequer and Audit Department (EAD), the government department responsible for auditing the accounts of other departments and public bodies. The National Audit Office (NAO) was established on 1 January 1984 under the National Audit Act 1983 from the EAD, under the direction of the Comptroller and Auditor General (C&AG), an officer of Parliament who reports to the

Committee on the expenditure of, and the promotion of economy, efficiency and effectiveness in, designated civil service departments and other public sector organisations receiving 50% or more of their funding from public funds.

While the Act specifically refuses the C&AG the right to "question the merits of the policy objectives" of any organisation it audits, the C&AG carries out several types of audit under the general objectives of assuring Parliament that public money has been spent for the purposes Parliament intended, improving financial control in the organisation it audits, improving value obtained from the resources made available by Parliament and improving the techniques and quality of public sector audit.

NAO has about 950 staff of which about 200 are administrative and related staff and is divided into five operational areas. The amounts involved are over £150 billion, mainly accounted for in the annual Appropriation Accounts (which also includes C&AG's views on specific items of expenditure). There are over 500 bodies involved and this type of audit takes up over 50% of NAO's time. The audited Accounts are laid before Parliament and may be examined by PAC which has a membership of up to 15 MPs and is chaired by an Opposition MP. It has powers to send for persons, papers and records. The Committee takes evidence primarily from Departmental Accounting Officers (or Chief Executives of Next Steps Agencies and other public bodies) and other relevant officials. C&AG may brief the Chair in confidence on issues of, for example, national security and PAC may elect not to publish such information ("sidelining"). The NAO's strong working relationship with PAC, whose members are aware of the attention the media accords to evidence of administrative malpractice, waste or misconduct, and an effective follow-up strategy to monitor committee recommendations for reform (and departmental promises on implementation), has provided one effective means of charting administrative change in action.

In addition to the certification audits and within the framework of NAO's strategic plan come the VFM studies, the Value For Money audits that pursue the issues of economy, effectiveness and efficiency. These are published in greenbacked reports, the "Green Glossies", and presented to Parliament. They offer a more detailed assessment of departmental activities than Appropriation Accounts and provide the opportunity to comment on the basis for, or financial consequences of, policy decisions and legislation the C&AG believes Parliament should know or may wish to review. VFM usually involves the study of those organisations through general surveys of departments every four or five years to review areas involving major resources and potential risks for achieving good value for money, to highlight areas for in-depth investigations. NAO collects and analyses information on objectives, activities, plans, resources, procedures and so on. Between reviews an annual marking takes place to identify changes in expenditure or activities and collect up-to-date key information toward an annual plan. VFM investigations fall into four broad areas: selective investigations of signs of possible serious waste, extravagance, inefficiency, ineffectiveness or weaknesses in control; major broad-based investigations of a whole body, or of important activities, projects or programmes to confirm satisfactory arrangements or uncover material weaknesses; major reviews of standard managerial operations ("good housekeeping" examinations); and small-scale investigations.

Similar changes have been made to the local government sector external audit when the District Audit Service's monopoly was ended in the early 1980s with the creation of an Audit Commission following the 1982 Local Government Finance Act, with three functions: to appoint auditors to 450 English and Welsh local authorities; to promote economy, efficiency and effectiveness as the means of assessing how well they use their funds to provide services; to report on the impact of central government actions on local authorities' ability to operate effectively. Auditors now include the large accountancy firms who have been identified by the Commission as, geographically, centres of excellence in a 30:70 split with the District Audit Service. In 1990 the Commission's remit was extended to encompass the National Health Service. The Commission agrees the auditors, establishes the fee, which is the same for both District Audit Service and private sector firms, and lays down the minimum audit time for each local authority.

Centrally the Commission has a number of special studies projects which either offer Commission comments on general management issues or areas of specific services. The studies work on the principles of ensuring widespread coverage of auditable activity by tackling high expenditure, specialised activities or differences in performance (to make added-value proposals) and to promote change, as well as assessing the impact of its own recommendations. A study takes about 18 months, using a team-based approach, through stages of initial research and study specifications, data collection, full-scale studies in a sample of volunteer authorities, publication of a report and, finally, development of an audit guide which provides a methodology benchmark for audit, good practice and performance standards as well as providing a means of comparison between organisations.

At District level the focus is on financial and VFM work. The District Audit Service is spread across seven regions, each with four District

Auditors, each heading three audit teams with six to 14 staff each. A region might have around 100 to 120 staff but there are no geographic patches in the sense that each District Auditor's teams may be spread throughout a region. Part of the audit function includes formal responsibility for assessing procedures and activities for the prevention of fraud and corruption, laying down both responsibilities and procedures on the basis that, although "the resources available to the auditor have to be put to best effect and the prevention and detection of fraud and irregularities is only one of many claims on audit time . . . the integrity of public funds is at all times a matter of general concern and the auditor should be aware that this function is seen to be an important safeguard".

The external auditor therefore is required to plan the audit, as in the case of District Audit, on the basis that

> there is a reasonable expectation of detecting material misstatements in the statement of accounts resulting from fraud and irregularities. Thus, the auditor should endeavour to identify and give any special attention to those activities of the authority which are particularly exposed to the risk of fraud and irregularities which, if present, could result in a material effect on the finances of the authority or a material misstatement in the statement of accounts . . . in the review on internal control, in the testing of transactions, and the review of published and other statistics, the auditor should be alert constantly to the possibility of fraud and irregularities. Management's attention should be drawn to any weakness in internal control which facilities fraud and irregularities and to those activities which call for occasional deterrent spot checks by management.

In the case of corruption, for example, the external audit requirements are explicit in terms of determining the responsibility: "it is the duty of the authority to take reasonable steps to limit the possibility of corrupt practices; and it is the responsibility of the auditor to review the adequacy of the measures taken by the authority, to test compliance and to draw attention to any weaknesses or omissions". This means that the external auditor has formalised approaches to risk and control; these include "reasonable steps to limit the possibility of corrupt practices", the role of internal audit to provide assurance and the warning that, in the public interest, any evidence of corruption may be "referred for further investigation by the appropriate body which according to the circumstances might be the authority or the police".

While the Audit Commission carries out national studies, its auditors work to their clients rather than to the Audit Commission as NAO does to

PAC. On the other hand, the Audit Commission's auditors have no requirement to discuss their reports prior to submission and have a number of legally-determined means for publicly identifying and penalising financial wrongdoing. Both sets of auditors have demonstrated their capability and capacity to uncover mismanagement and misconduct during substantial changes to the provision and delivery of public services.

Fifteen Years of Change and Organisational Turbulence
The short reference in the 1979 Conservative manifesto, that the reduction of waste, bureaucracy and overgovernment would yield substantial savings, which was a general phrase to deal with the cost and size of government has been elevated to a blueprint for reform. Unlike the Fulton Report which proposed management reform within a given public service framework, the process was and is the continuous reduction of the size and cost of the public sector with an underlying belief that the private sector approach provided the model to follow for the delivery of public services. Sir Robin Butler, Head of the civil service, told a recent Political Studies Association conference that he did not know what the final shape of the civil service would be: "it is not unusual, I guess, for an organisation in the process of evolution not to know what its final state will be" (Dynes and Walker 1995). The Rayner scrutiny reviews, intended to look at specific civil service activities to encourage simplification, streamlining and better procedures, were followed by the Financial Management Initiative (FMI), encouraged by the Treasury and Civil Service Committee's enthusiasm for the introduction of programme management expenditure, and line management budgetary control and responsibility. FMI sought to introduce a financial and management information system as the basis for continuous good management practice through cost awareness and responsible and devolved management. Its intention was for more measures of achievement; targets for individual managers who would be held accountable for achieving an agreed level of performance. The patchiness and slowness of the changes within the civil service, the ingrained Whitehall culture, the lack of ministerial interest in systematic reform, the lack of effective devolution for responsibility over costs and the reported frustration below senior management level and the low level of financial savings, led to the Efficiency Unit, the organisation carrying on the focus of the work begun by the scrutiny reviews, to produce the Next Steps report in 1988 as the vehicle to overcome the lack of urgency and alter "cultural attitudes and behaviour of government so that continuous improvement becomes a widespread and inbuilt feature of it" (Efficiency Unit 1988).

Its main proposals were for departments to be shrunk and to focus on policy and advice for ministers while the bulk of the executive functions would pass to delivery agencies, not necessarily staffed by civil servants or working to civil service pay and conditions of service, which would create the organisational context for cultural change from public to private sector values. This approach was echoed in different ways, but with the same intention, across the public sector as the 1987 General Election heralded radical structural reform (internal markets, devolution, compulsory competitive tendering (CCT), local management of schools(LMS), privatisation and so on) across the public sector to also create the context for similar change.

The intended shift in culture from caution and risk-avoidance to risk-taking (Metcalfe and Richards 1990), from the anonymous application of rules to individual, responsive and dynamic management control (Willson 1991) has created "significant amounts of organisational turbulence"(Flynn 1992) within which public officials were required to take on, without substantial training, new, often complex, managerial roles, including inter-agency negotiation, political accountability, customer service delivery, competitive tendering, budgetary and financial management, property management, works services, purchasing, locally determined pay and conditions and new technology. Not only have these processes throughout the public sector been subject to the speed, purpose and complexity of the change by organisations and within organisations, but change has itself thrown up a number of issues such as job security or, conversely, the opportunities offered by buy-outs and privatisation, and the sometimes conflicting objectives of speed of delivery, cost-cutting and performance by results against those of due process, procedure and precedent. The development of a management culture within a public service context, and the consequential changes in approach to work, performance and integrity, would, it could be assumed, also require learning processes, rather than assumptions, to reassess and develop existing public sector standards of conduct but to which little attention was given.

While the Efficiency Unit's 1988 report acknowledged that organisational and cultural change would require a redefinition of ministerial accountability and the accountability of agencies to PAC and other select committees, it was dismissive of the existing means of monitoring any adverse effects of change, saying that: "pressure from parliament, the Public Accounts Committee and the media tends to concentrate on alleged impropriety or incompetence, and making political points, rather than on demanding evidence of steadily improving efficiency and effectiveness".

The report, however, also stated that the role of the "centre of government" included a requirement "to set and police essential rules on propriety for the public service in carrying out its essential functions". In a context in which the Treasury and Civil Service Committee was praising departments for their "hands-off approach" to agencies and inviting them to pursue "cultural change" and "a large scale re-writing of the rule-book"(Treasury and Civil Service Committee 1989–90) so ministers and senior civil servants' approaches to standards of conduct was an over-reliant faith in self-sustaining "common standards" across a "unified but not a uniform Civil Service" (Treasury and Civil Service Committee 1988–89). In 1990 Richard Luce, the government minister responsible for the civil service, referred to the need, within the framework of the maximum possible delegation of authority, to ensure that the "very important principles and traditions" were upheld in relation to "the impartiality of the service, to the high standards of propriety in the Service, to the maintenance of principles of accountability within the Service . . ." (Treasury and Civil Service Committee 1989–90). The Government itself has insisted that Next Steps offered "all future governments an effective and adaptable Civil service, with all its traditional values of propriety and impartiality intact . . ." (The Government Reply to the Seventh Report from the Treasury and Civil Service Committee 1990–91 1991). Indeed, as late as July 1994, the Government were suggesting that various initiatives, such as the Citizens Charter, FMI and Next Steps agencies had in themselves "promoted greater transparency" and strengthened "accountability to both Parliament and the public". It also argued that the existing Civil Service Management Code was sufficient to "ensure that the defining principles and standards of the Civil Service (were) not relaxed and they continue to be mandatory for all departments and agencies"(The Civil Service 1994, 1995).

Nevertheless, the environment in which traditional public service standards of conduct existed reflected general areas of internal organisational or procedural weaknesses, including: weak guidance on standards of conduct or non-compliance with procedures; management indifference or ignorance; inadequate financial and management information systems; lax working practices; poor staff relations; sub-organisational autonomy; overlapping functions; excessive discretion in the performance of official duties; inadequate recruitment, promotion and training policies; prolonged or overclose contact with private sector values, personnel and practices which could result in the exploitation of weak public sector procedures and standards. The speed and direction of devolved managerial autonomy, together with the promotion of an entrepreneurial culture and of privatisation as an goal for public sector organisations, have raised further questions about the vulnerability of public sector officials and organisations, the weakening of the public sector ethos and ethical environment, the impact of private sector perspectives within a public sector context, the inevitable balance between public service and personal benefit and the implications of change on existing but ill-defined relationships of accountability, monitoring and control. In addition to the effects of existing organisational weaknesses are now added the effects of dysfunctional change, including: the search for job security; poor management control; misinterpretation of performance rewards; over-ambitious projects; new management culture; the failure to enforce, or police, regulations and procedures; the potential for conflict of interest between personal benefit and public service; and the inadequacy of scrutiny and oversight. In such circumstances, as Jenny Harrow and Roy Gillett put it, many public officials may have become involved in such activities as a result of a "misunderstanding among public servants about the quasi-private sector environment . . . (and) . . . inaccurate perceptions of private sector values and practices" (Harrow and Gillett 1994) as the following examples show.

- The Forward Civil Service catering department's attention to possible privatisation led to a failure to maintain financial control and led to allegations of deals with suppliers, massaged performance figures, fraud, conflict-of-interest and tax evasion (Committee of Public Accounts (a) 1992–93).
- West Wiltshire District Council's in-house development of software programmes were subject to a management buy-out [MBO], just on the point when the Council was likely to generate substantial licence income, against a background, alleged the District Auditor, of: serious weaknesses in the Council's committee structures; the failure to take impartial advice; inadequate reporting procedures; the apparent absence of detailed working papers and documentation; potential conflict of interests among senior officials; and the naivety of councillors (Doig (a) 1995).
- The £9.4 million Ministry of Defence efficiency incentive scheme which should have benefitted the defence community as a whole was used for high volume, low cost items of personal or social benefit because of a lack of guidance on how and for whom the money should have been spent (Committee of Public Accounts (b) 1992–93).

- The Foreign and Commonwealth Office's new computerised accounting was less than successful for operational and other reasons at a time when there was "a complete turnover in bookkeeping staff . . . when major changes were taking place" (Committee of Public Accounts 1990–91).
- West Midlands Regional Health Authority's [RHA] appointment of a director to bring a new "culture" with him led to the hiring of management consultants at substantial cost allegedly at variance with standing orders and financial regulations to install that culture; the allegations of "grave weaknesses in management and accountability" were supplemented by further concerns over an unorthodox £7 million consultancy contract to introduce an electronic trading system, a failed MBO underwritten by the Authority, loans to a company in financial difficulties, the employment of outside consultants for staff appointments, the withholding of funds owed to District Health Authorities and various unusual arrangements concerning terms and conditions of service (Committee of Public Accounts (c) 1992–93).
- Wessex RHA's expenditure of over £40 million on a sophisticated IT strategy under the guidance of its consultants who also ended up as its suppliers led to the District Auditor reporting that the RHA's budgetary control was so weak that "it took until half way through the following financial year before the total commitment for the earlier year could be estimated with any accuracy". The District Auditor also alleged: poorly-defined consultancies were handed out on the basis of verbal agreements reached at informal meetings; contract procedures were ignored; no internal audit work was carried out between 1985–89 (when £38 million was spent) and no attempt was made to ensure value for money. The use of outside consultants deprived the RHA of experienced in-house staff and created potential conflicts of interest, while the volume of work involved in monitoring the activities of consultants invariably outstripped the RHA's capacity and capabilities for effective monitoring to the point where mismanagement and the potential for more serious misconduct existed (Committee of Public Accounts (d) 1992–93).
- The Welsh Development Agency, among other criticisms, was taken to task for appointing a director of marketing who had previous convictions for deception, and using public funds to pay consultants to consider options for the future of the Agency, including privatisation, which were concealed within the Agency's accounts (Committee of Public Accounts (e) 1992–93).

- The Sports Council has been criticised for "weakened accountability for and control over publicly funded assets and services . . . made more serious by the lack of a clear arms length relationship between the bodies forming the Council Group and inadequate arrangements to prevent conflicts of duty or interest or the appearance of such conflicts" after the Council set up a number of trading companies with staff and members involved in the Council and its commercial companies. (National Audit Office 1994; Committee of Public Accounts 1994–95).
- The National Rivers Authority hired a private sector company in 1990 to handle its relocation to leased premises in Bristol but its senior staff responsible for the project "had no background in project management". Its vetting, contract rules, financial supervision, and control over sub-contractors were all inadequate, with the attendant risks of financial misconduct (Committee of Public Accounts 1991–92).
- The Export Credit Guarantee Department lost a net of up to £30 million on loans to an overseas company to buy two oil rigs built in Scotland. Those who made the original decisions did not inform senior management and did not check the creditworthiness of the borrower. There was poor recordkeeping, Government accounting rules were ignored and allegations of fraud were not reported to appropriate ECGD unit because it was "new" (Committee of Public Accounts (a) 1993–94).

Conclusion: First or Last Defence Against Fraud?

The detailed understanding that regular audit work across the organisation brings, the in-depth studies of parts of the organisation, the risk and materiality work and the independent reporting to an independent agency does allow public sector external auditors to be more demanding in their inquiries and more forthright in their reports. These features (independence from the organisations audited, a wider role in audit and a greater emphasis on reporting to the stakeholders) are, according to CIPFA (*Independent* (e) 1995), key differences to private sector audit. While acknowledging the variations between sectors, there is also a realisation that the increasing involvement of the private sector in the delivery of public services may expose such companies to the stringency of public sector audit. While government is resisting the attempts of the NAO to access the books of the companies (Doig (b) 1995) there are moves in the private sector to seek to achieve some of the advantages that the public sector external audit currently has (*The Times* 1995; *Independent on Sunday* 1995). It remains to be seen whether they are also prepared to pay the price, not only with the ending of the informal relations with their employers and the hands-off approach of their professional bodies, but also with the possibility of others controlling their fees and provision of other lucrative financial services, in return raising the figure of detected frauds and earning the gratitude of the shareholders. On the other hand, the crucial role of external audit, even in the public sector, as the first as well as the last line of defence against fraud, waste and mismanagement is further underlined by the lack of a suitable alternative as both the first, or preventative, defence or as the last, or investigative, defence against fraud.

It may be argued that the responsibility for ensuring the effectiveness of procedures and systems, and reporting on their capabilities for the prevention and detection of fraud or corruption, to management should lie with internal audit. In 1987 the Comptroller and Auditor General reviewed his predecessor's comments in 1981 on the NHS internal audit that generally

> there was a lack of audit planning and reporting; the coverage of computer systems, capital expenditure and family practitioner services was deficient; and in England staff numbers were below those recommended by regional treasurers to achieve satisfactory financial audit standards. In Scotland, health boards' internal audit units had contributed little to the maintenance of financial control.

He himself had to report that, five years later, "most had not achieved the defined minimum acceptable level of audit coverage" (National Audit Office (a) 1987). At the same time he also noted his precedessor's comments on internal audit in central government:

> the overall standard of internal audit in central government was substantially below the level needed to fulfil its recommended role. Weaknesses noted included lack of professionalism among staff; fragmented responsibility for duties, structuring and staffing; inadequate computer audit capability; and a general failure to appreciate the benefit of a strong internal audit.

Again, five years later, he was reporting that, while the Internal Audit Development Division of the Treasury was bringing reform to internal audit and that internal audit staff were carrying out their work in a way that would reveal significant defects in internal control systems, the C&AG noted that departmental internal audit "still have some way to go to achieve an adequate standard . . ." (National Audit Office (b) 1987).

If the means to promote the prevention and detection of fraud internally is problematical, so is that of investigation and prosecution. There are some

125,000 police officers in 43 forces in England and Wales. The police are only one organisation (and not in any case a national organisation) in a landscape of

> a mixture of police forces, regulatory bodies, governmental and quasi-governmental agencies, involved in policing and law enforcement duties of one sort or another. Such bodies may operate in the public sphere, in the private sphere, or across both ... rigorous classification is probably an impossible task since the functions, practices, jurisdictions, and legal powers of the various bodies overlap in potentially complex ways (Johnston 1992 p115).

In 1992, only 770 of the 125,000 police officers were designated as fraud squads officers of whom one-third were based in London; another 210 have been employed on complex fraud cases such as mortgage fraud. While the amounts of money involved in fraud cases have been inflated by cases such as those of Barlow Clowes, Maxwell and Polly Peck, the Serious Fraud Office and the Fraud Investigation Group of the Crown Prosecution Service were dealing with cases where nearly £10 billion had been stolen or was at risk while large fraud squads such as those of the West Yorkshire and West Midlands police forces have substantial annual caseloads running to many millions of pounds where the average amount at risk is over £500,000 (Levi 1993 pp7–12). The mismatch between the cost of fraud and the number of officers devoted to its investigation and prosecution reflects the more traditional (and political) agenda of public safety and public order and crime against the individual. Furthermore the primacy of that agenda has caused a number of police forces to question the resources and time devoted to fraud investigations. One government department has admitted that it "sometimes finds it hard to obtain the cooperation and assistance it needs as police authorities throughout the country find it necessary to deploy their forces on matters judged to be of a higher priority", reporting that at least one major force had warned the Department and other organisations that "it may need to limit its activities to the maintenance of law and order and to crime against private individuals, so that organisations must fend for themselves"(Lidstone *et al* 1980 p51). Furthermore, that attitude has in part been responsible for many public sector organisations undertaking quasi-police roles (Doig (c) 1995) to the point where there is the concern that any emphasis on a predominantly investigative and prosecutorial approach raises the question of how far the public sector should go to investigate fraud. One review at the end of the 1980s warned of one government department's approach: "there must also be a recognition that the boundary between what is proper to police action and what is legitimately the responsibility of the Department does not get redrawn as a consequence. In our view that boundary has already moved too far in the wrong direction".

The role of the external auditor in preventing and detecting fraud, as well as encouraging preventive controls and procedures, is pivotal for a public sector where both the Audit Commission (Audit Commission 1993) and PAC (Committee of Public Accounts (b) 1993–94) have noted the impact of change on management's ability to ensure the implementation and operation of such controls and procedures, where there is slow development of internal audit as an effective source of assurance and scrutiny and where there is continuing pressure on police resources and priorities. In such circumstances in the public sector at least and for the moment, external audit may be the first and last line against fraud, waste and mismanagement. As the role of the private sector in the delivery of public services increases so the performance of public sector external audit may also provide examples of best practice that private sector private audit may wish to emulate both for their role in the public sector but also in seeking to deal with the excesses of the 1980s in the private sector.

References

Adams, J.R. and Frantz, D. (1993) *A Full Service Bank* London, Simon and Schuster
Adonis, A. (1990) *Parliament Today* Manchester, Manchester University Press
Audit Commission (1993) *Protecting the Public Purse: Combatting Fraud and Corruption in Local Government* London, HMSO
Cadbury, Report of the Committee on the Financial Aspects of Corporate Governance (1992) Gee & Co Ltd
The Civil Service: Continuity and Change (1994) Cm 2627, London, HMSO
The Civil Service: Taking Forward Continuity and Change (1995) Cm 2748 London HMSO
Clarke, M. (1986) *Regulating The City* OUP, Milton Keynes
Clarke, M. (1990) *Business Crime* Cambridge Polity Press
Committee of Public Accounts. (1990–91) *36th Report* London HMSO
Committee of Public Accounts (1991–92) *23rd Report* London HMSO
Committee of Public Accounts (a) (1992–93) *48th Report* London HMSO
Committee of Public Accounts (b) (1992–93) *28th Report* London HMSO
Committee of Public Accounts (c) (1992–93) *57th Report* London HMSO

Committee of Public Accounts (d) (1992–93) *63rd Report* London HMSO
Committee of Public Accounts (e) (1992–93) *47th Report* London HMSO
Committee of Public Accounts (1993–94) *5th Report* London HMSO
Committee of Public Accounts (1993–94) *8th Report* London HMSO
Committee of Public Accounts (1994–95) *2nd Report* London, HMSO
Doig, A. (a) (1995) "No Reason For Complacency? Organisational Change and Probity in Local Government" *Local Government Studies*
Doig, A. (b) (1995) "Mixed Signals? Public Sector Change and the Proper Conduct of Public Business" *Public Administration* Vol 73 No 2 pp191-212
Doig, A. (c) (1995) "Changing Public Sector Approaches to Fraud" *Public Money and Management* Vol 15 No 1 pp19-24
Dynes, M. and Walker, D. (1995) *The New British State* London Times Books
Efficiency Unit (1988) *Improving Management in Government: The Next Steps* London HMSO
Ernst and Young (1995) *Fraud: The Unmanaged Risk 1994/95* London Ernst and Young
Flynn, R. (1992) *Structures of Control in Health Management* London Routledge
Gardner, D. (1995) *Auditor Liability: A Case to Answer* Liverpool, Liverpool Business School Working Paper Series No 1
The Government Reply to the Seventh Report from the Treasury and Civil Service Committee 1990–91 (1991) London HMSO
Harrow, J. and Gillett, R. (1994) "The Proper Conduct of Public Business" *Public Money and Management* Vol 14 No 2
Independent (a) (1993) 18 May
Independent (b) (1994) 30 October
Independent (c) (1994) 13 September
Independent (d) (1995) 5 and 6 May
Independent (e) (1995) 25 January
Independent on Sunday (1995) 14 May
Johnston, L (1992) *The Rebirth of Private Policing* London Routledge
Le Quesne (1988) *Barlow Clowes* Report of Sir Godfray le Quesne, London HMSO
Lever, L. (1992) *The Barlow Clowes Affair* London Coronet
Levi, M. (1987) *Regulating Fraud: White-Collar Crime and the Criminal Process* London Routledge
Levi, M. (1993) *The Investigation, Prosecution and Trial of Serious Fraud,* Royal Commission on Criminal Justice Research Study No 14 London HMSO
Lidstone, K. W., Hogg, R., Sutcliffe, F. "Prosecutions by Private Individuals and non-Police Agencies" *Royal Commission on Criminal Procedure, Research Study 10* London HMSO

The Listener (1988) 25 February

Metcalfe, L. and Richards, S. (1990) *Improving Public Management* London Sage

National Audit Office (a) (1987) *Internal Audit in the Health Service* London HMSO HCP 314

National Audit Office (b) (1987) *Internal Audit in Central Government* London, HMSO HCP 313

National Audit Office (1994) *The Sports Council.* London HMSO

Observer (a) (1992) 9 February

Observer (b) (1992) 25 October

Observer (c) (1992) 15 March

Observer (d) (1992) 23 August

Observer (e) (1992) 15 March

Observer (f) (1992) 23 August

The Sunday Times (1991) 29 December

The Times (1995) 11 May

Treasury and Civil Service Committee (1988–89) *5th Report* HC 348 London HMSO

Treasury and Civil Service Committee (1989–90) *8th Report* HC

Treasury and Civil Service Committee (1991–2) *4th Report* London HMSO

Willson, M. (1991) "Contracting Corruption" *Local Government Studies* 17, 3

Wilson, J. and Doig, A. (1995) "Untangling the Threads of Sleaze: The Slide into Nolan" *Parliamentary Affairs* 48, 4 pp562-78

7

Resource Accounting in the Public Sector

John Wilson

Introduction

The public sector has been subjected to particularly close scrutiny for two decades. Since the mid-1970s attention has focused upon the scale of its activity and the degree to which it can demonstrate economy, efficiency and effectiveness in the use of resources. Insofar as services continue to be supplied by the public sector, they are done so within an increasingly competitive environment. Efficiency and competitiveness need to be measured. This is problematic given the nature of much public sector activity, but central to the exercise is the measurement of the use of finite resources to establish the "true cost" of services. "True cost" is itself a misleading expression "given the numerous cost concepts, such as opportunity cost, marginal cost and sunk costs" (Mayston 1992a p231) but the search for it has entailed accounting for the use of capital assets.

Establishing true cost also provides a means of improving accountability. However, this assumes that the financial information is meaningful and comprehensible. The issue of resource accounting is closely linked to these wider issues of financial reporting and accountability (see, for instance, Mayston 1992b). This chapter considers the debate concerning resource accounting in the public sector and, in doing so, focuses particularly upon local government.

Public Sector Accounting

The components parts of the public sector, central government, local government and public corporations, traditionally adopted accounting policies which differed not only from each other but also from those adopted by the private sector. The accounts of public corporations, notably the nationalised industries, tended to reflect best commercial practice but this was not true of central government, including the National Health Service (NHS), and local government. The two underlying reasons for this are their different objectives and the nature of their output.

Government departments, local authorities and the NHS do not exist to make a profit but rather to provide a vast range of services available to all. They are provided irrespective of whether or not they can be demonstrated to be "profitable". The provision of public services including education, defence, social services, healthcare, public broadcasting, law and order and so on is not dependent upon the probability of profit or the need to reward equity capital. Private sector profit maximisation, therefore, can be contrasted with public sector service provision and this distinction influenced accounting policy. There was no need to achieve a profit or to consider how such a measure of performance could be demonstrated within the context of, for instance, the Ministry of Defence, a District Health Authority or a Water Authority.

There is also less need to pursue commercial practice given that much public service output is not sold within the marketplace. It is important to appreciate that some output is priced, for example gas, electricity, and rail travel, and the cost of other services is paid for indirectly through taxation; but pricing to recover costs was irrelevant for many services, for example health and education. The emphasis was traditionally on standards of probity, stewardship and accountability.

These two fundamental differences with the private sector shaped the nature of public sector accounting practices but, in considering these practices, a broad distinction could previously have been made between organisations which adopted cash accounting and those which adopted accruals accounting. Cash accounting records only cash inflows and outflows and, consequently, the final accounts are simply summarised cash books. This means that there are no balance sheets, no assets or liabilities, no debtors, creditors or opening and closing stock figures. The most significant example of cash accounting can be found in the accounts of central government departments. These reveal simply an excess of receipts over payments or vice versa.

The three main merits of cash accounting (see Jones and Pendlebury 1988) are simplicity (they can be easily understood and interpreted), low cost (easy to administer and do not require technical expertise) and factual accuracy (that is, they are not based on subjective judgments). However, cash accounting suffers from two fundamental and related defects.

First, there is no measure of capital. The absence of information concerning assets and liabilities creates serious problems in considering the financial value of an organisation. Second, there is no measure of income. This also means it is not possible to assess performance by the usual commercial criterion of calculating a return on capital. Jones and Pendlebury (1988 p159) summarise these problems.

> An excess of receipts over payments cannot be called income because receipts might include capital receipts. Similarly, an excess of payments over receipts cannot be called a loss because the payment might include the acquisition of assets. There is no opportunity to compare income with capital to yield a return on capital figure which is typically used as a measure of a business's performance. Indeed, there is no opportunity to use an income figure in any way as a comparative measure of performance.

These two defects, inter alia, precluded meaningful performance measures but they also prevented any evaluation of capital consumption. Misleading conclusions could, therefore, be drawn from the cash accounts at year-end in that they would not reflect the impact on the total capital stock of the policies pursued or services delivered in any particular year. Selling public sector assets, for instance, reduces the capital stock and means that the organisation is denied the future value of the asset. In the accounts, however, substantial receipts will be recorded and a distorted impression given.

The accounts are also distorted by excluding receipts and payments which relate to the year of the account but which are actually recorded in the year the cash transaction takes place. An example of this would be the credit purchase of fuel used in year one but paid for in year two. The effect is to under-record the cost of service provision in year one and over-record it in year two.

The disadvantages associated with cash accounting has led to increased demands for the adoption of accruals accounting, the two most common forms of which are historic cost accounting and current cost accounting. Accruals accounting essentially involves matching revenue and costs to the actual period to which they relate. Central to this is the depreciation of capital assets, except for those which are not depreciable, namely land. Under historic cost accounting, non-depreciable assets are shown in the balance sheet as the value of the initial investment; other assets are shown net of depreciation. With current cost accounting, non-depreciable assets are shown at their current value, which would normally be their replacement cost. Depreciable assets are shown at their replacement cost less the cumulative depreciation.

The main problem with accruals accounting is that it is based on inherently subjective assumptions. How much depreciation to charge and how to value assets' replacement cost, for instance, are important questions but can be answered in different ways. There are also problems with historic cost accounting during inflationary periods, as the accounts will not present an accurate picture. The value of assets, for instance, may be understated (current value exceeding historic cost) whilst the net profit figure would be overstated (the result of depreciation being based on historic cost rather than current value). Nonetheless, the principle of matching revenues and costs to the correct period is sound and allows the true cost of any activity to be quantified or at least approximated. Accruals accounting, therefore, involving as it does measurement of capital and depreciation, facilitates assessment of economic performance and comparisons over time and with other similar departments or organisations.

The emphasis on establishing the true cost of services and the related emphases on economy, efficiency and effectiveness, have resulted in a critical evaluation of public sector accounting practices. The need for this has been further reinforced by the commercialisation of much public sector activity and the introduction of market forces. Where it has not been possible to introduce conventional markets, quasi-markets have been established, as in the NHS. The extensive application of market principles has necessitated changes in accounting practices to ensure they reflect, and are appropriate for, the changed environment within which public services are provided. Increased commercialisation has been accompanied by increased adoption of commercial accounting techniques. Accruals accounting is replacing cash accounting and accounting for the existence and use of capital assets is now the norm.

The broad distinction, therefore, between those public sector bodies which adopt cash accounting and those which adopt accruals accounting is increasingly blurred. Similarly, the differences between public sector accounting practice and that of the private sector are becoming less.

Resource Accounting – Central Government and the NHS

In the Budget Statement 30 Nov 1993, the Chancellor announced changes to central government accounting and stated that accruals-based resource accounting and budgeting would be introduced. He described current arrangements as "archaic" and said " . . . the time has come to move to a system of accounting which identifies more clearly the cost of resources. This will put departments onto a similar accounting basis to commercial organisations and many other parts of the public sector" (HMSO 1993 p93). Some commentators, for example Davis (1993), view this as fundamentally important and believe it will facilitate the quantification of the true cost of delivering services. Others (e.g. Jones 1996) are opposed and believe it to be unnecessary and attempts to apply it to central government will prove counter-productive. However, the Chancellor published a White Paper (HMSO 1995) which set out the new accounting arrangements for central government.

The Chancellor's innovation is consistent with the Government's bias towards private sector practice, but as Henley (1992 p94) points out:

> Most government activities accounted for in cash terms are quite different from trading operations where it is essential for survival to calculate expenditure and fix prices with adequate regard to the full annual costs, capital and current, being incurred. Capital expenditure on a warship or the new British Library should not be incurred without applying appropriate criteria, and it makes the same kind of demand on the construction and engineering industries as capital spending by business. The resulting equipment should be run as efficiently as possible, but it does not result in a stream of saleable products to generate profit, and the criteria for judging it will not be commercial criteria.

This illustrates that the distinction between the private sector and some aspects of public sector activity should not be ignored nor can it be eradicated. To advocate the application of best commercial practice to all aspects of the public sector is politically dogmatic rather than technically cogent. Nonetheless, it also needs to be appreciated that the utilisation of finite resources by the public sector may result in an opportunity cost in terms of foregone private sector output (there are also competing public sector claims) and it is important to demonstrate that public sector activity and output is compatible with productive and allocative efficiency. This is particularly relevant to the NHS given the magnitude of the expenditure involved.

Accounting arrangements in the NHS were completely at variance with best commercial practice, no more so than in respect of capital. Expenditure on capital items was written-off in the year incurred. There were no balance sheets, no depreciation of fixed assets and no repayment of principal. Funding was received from central government and capital was treated as a "free good". Perrin (1992 p233) points out that ". . . it had long been argued that receiving capital as a free good could lead to excessive use or waste of capital on individual projects" and, unsurprisingly, these arrangements were debated over a period of several years (see AHST 1985; Lapsley 1986; Mellet 1988). The argument that depreciation and interest charges would ensure increased efficiency in the use of capital gradually became accepted and a system of charging for capital was introduced with effect from April 1991 (Department of Health 1989).

A new definition of capital has been introduced to cover all tangible assets and the use of them now incurs capital charges which comprise a 6% rate of return and depreciation charges. The annual interest charge is 6% of the current value of assets. All fixed assets, excluding land, which cost £5000 or more are depreciated on a straight line basis. Land incurs an interest charge but not a depreciation charge. Land and buildings are revalued every five years by the District Valuer with valuations updated on an annual basis in the interim by means of index adjustments. A distinction is also made between assets with "variable lives", that is the asset's life expectancy may increase or reduce depending upon the valuer's estimation, and those with "fixed lives" (published by the Department of Health). Land and buildings are the main examples of assets with variable lives; furniture, vehicles, office equipment, etc are categorised as fixed.

Capital, therefore, is no longer a "free good" within the NHS. Balance sheets are produced, assets identified and depreciation shown. Capital charges that is, depreciation and a required 6% return on net relevant assets are also used to determine prices within the internal market. Prices set by providers within the market, should be based on full-cost recovery including the depreciation charge and a rate of return on capital (interest charge, in recognition of the opportunity cost element).

However, there are problems arising from the measures which have been introduced. Efficient use of capital may be encouraged, as inefficient use or excessive expansion will result in increased capital charges which will reduce the competitiveness of any provider unit. In this situation, assets may be disposed of and/or "throughput" increased (thereby reducing average capital cost per unit). However, as Mellett (1990) points out, the latter may not be possible if a hospital is working at or near full capacity. High capital costs and near-capacity working can simultaneously occur, for instance, where land values are disproportionately high. There is a need, therefore, to differentiate between high capital costs caused by inefficiency and those caused by extraneous factors. However, there is a further need to differentiate between volume variance (such as too much land held) and price variance (current value per unit of area). Where high capital charges are mainly the result of the latter, complications occur as to the ability of the provider unit to compete given the framework within which it must operate. Mellett (1990 p281) correctly states

> . . . the private sector certainly has the freedom to use those accounting and pricing policies which best promote its objectives. Therefore, the NHS units will have to recover in their prices both interest and depreciation charges based on current values while, if it wished, the private sector could use marginal cost, or just above, especially in the short-term, to gain a competitive advantage or possibly just to show relatively low-cost figures.

Dixon (1993 p58) also states that although managers will have become aware of the cost of their capital equipment, "there is a substantial difference between the valuation procedures in the NHS and those employed by the private sector" thereby making more difficult the achievement of one of the aims of the capital accounting changes, which is "to set the NHS and private sector on a level playing field."

Local Government

In 1993 a revised version of a code of practice on local authority accounting was endorsed by the Accounting Standards Board (ASB) and thereby acquired the status of a Statement of Recommended Practice (SORP) (CIPFA 1993a). According to Evans (1993 pp44–45), the Head of CIPFA's Technical Division, "the changes to the balance sheet and revenue account required by the new SORP are the most significant changes in local authority accounting practice in the last 100 years."

The origin of the present debate concerning local authority capital accounting can be traced to the mid-1970s (though there have been periodic questions raised against its rationale since the beginning of the century; see, for instance, Coombs and Edwards 1992; Jones 1985; for a summary of the debate between 1975 and 1987 see CIPFA 1993b pp120–128). The method of accounting for capital adopted by local government was unique. It not only differed from commercial practice but also from that adopted elsewhere in the public sector. Historically, its rationale was a function of the need for political accountability. Local councillors could not simply spend money on behalf of their constituents in an effort to be returned to power by a grateful electorate. On the contrary, expenditure had to be financed. Capital schemes were normally financed by borrowing but the amounts borrowed and the interest payable were repaid by means of a property tax, in the form of rates, levied on the main beneficiaries of the expenditure, the local electorate. A system of accounting was adopted which recorded the annual debt charges, principal and interest, in the revenue account and these repayments influenced the rate levy. Excessive expenditure would necessarily entail an excessive tax burden and invite electoral retribution. Financial and political accountability were therefore inextricably linked by the relationship between finance and accounting.

This relationship was subsequently reinforced by the legal requirements which governed capital accounting and which meant that principal repayments were charged to the revenue account and treated as an operating expense. This differed from commercial practice whereby principal repayments are reflected in the balance sheet by using cash to reduce long-term liabilities. The operating expenses are shown as interest and depreciation and charged to the profit and loss account. For local authorities, however, the legal requirement to ensure an annual provision for the repayment of debt, with principal repayments rather than depreciation, cemented the link between capital cost and capital finance, an historic link rooted in political accountability.

However, problems and inconsistencies developed over time. A fundamental problem stemmed from the fact that not all capital expenditure was financed by borrowing; a local authority's assets could be financed by a variety of methods including revenue contributions, reserves (viz a Capital Fund) and grants. No charge equivalent to depreciation was debited to the revenue account in respect of assets financed directly from revenue or grants and no consistent policy had been adopted when assets had been financed from internal sources, such as Capital Fund (see Parkes 1989).

An additional complication arose from the fact that, though it was possible to borrow money for specific schemes, and earmarked for a particular purpose, and make the necessary accounting entries in the appropriate service revenue accounts, in reality, a local authority managed its loans centrally. The accounting arrangements for such central management have varied over time but, essentially, loans would be "pooled', a Loans Fund established and individual services would borrow from it. This "pooling" of a local authority's borrowings meant that the link between a specific asset and an external loan was broken and the recording of debt charges was a notional book-keeping exercise.

A report was issued by CIPFA (1983) which identified weaknesses in the existing system of accounting. To address the criticisms, a system of asset rentals was recommended whereby individual services would be charged a rental, professionally determined and regularly reviewed, for land and property occupied. Importantly, this would not affect the overall rate levy as the rentals charged would be credited to a central account and which in turn would offset the overall revenue requirement. This distinction between the charge to services and the charge to ratepayers constituted a decisive departure from past practice.

A further report was published by CIPFA (1984). This supported the principle of asset rents but experiments which had been conducted highlighted that, though appropriate for land and buildings, it was not particularly suitable for other assets, such as vehicles and plant. In addition, the process of valuation could be problematic, not least because authorities did not have definitive asset records.

In 1985, central government dissatisfaction with local authority accounts was evidenced by the publication of a Consultation Paper (DoE 1985) which sought to standardise and commercialise accounting practice. The Paper was subsequently withdrawn but the Government invited local authorities and the accounting profession to formulate their own proposals. CIPFA and the Audit Commission established a working party which published a consultative document in October 1986 (see Cook 1987) and was published as a Code of Practice in 1987 (CIPFA 1987), adopted with effect from 1 April 1987. This was an interim measure to be implemented until revised capital accounting recommendations were formulated and accepted. To this end, CIPFA established a Working Party which reported in September 1987 (CIPFA 1993b) and, as a result, a Capital Accounting Steering Group (CASG) was established the Final Report of which was published in 1990.

In the meantime, a legislative change occurred with the 1989 Local Government and Housing Act, which came into effect on 1 April 1990. Its detailed regulations are not relevant here, but it gave local authorities the option to abolish Loans Funds. In addition, Part 4 of the Act imposed new restrictions on the operation of local authorities' revenue accounts, established new controls over borrowing to finance capital expenditure and over the use of capital receipts. In effect, the Act, inter alia, transferred controls on capital spending to capital financing and sought to force local authorities into speedier repayment of external debt. Theoretically, from 1 April 1990, a local authority had complete discretion to spend any amount of money on capital schemes but the methods of financing were so tightly defined that the controls were much more effective than when they were based on capital spending.

The controls on methods of financing included the categorisation of borrowing, leasing, deferred purchase arrangements and all "creative" practices as "Credit Arrangements" and the establishment of a "Credit Limit" (Basic Credit Approval) by central government for each authority. In addition, capital receipts unapplied have to be retained in specified ratios and used for the repayment of loans (rather than financing new capital expenditure). Limits were also imposed on revenue contributions to capital. Early repayment of loans is achieved by use of capital receipts as given above and by minimum revenue provisions (MRPs) being debited to service revenue accounts as repayments to the Loans Pool. These replace the "principal" component of debt charges (shown as Debt Charges – MRP rather than Debt Charges – Principal) and are based on each authority's Credit Limit at the start of each year.

The Final Report of the CASG, which now had to reflect the requirements of the 1989 Act, was met with considerable opposition from local authorities, mainly on the grounds of practicability, cost (of the valuation exercise), timing (particularly relevant given the review of local government structures) and complexity, though their principles were already being applied in Direct Labour Organisation (DLO) – now generally referred to as Direct Service Organisations (DSOs) – rates of return statements. These concerns were considered by a Capital Accounting Working Group (CAWG), supplemented by a pilot study based on Solihull MBC and two additional "satellite" studies at St Edmonsdbury BC and London Borough of Croydon. CAWG's report was published in 1993 (CIPFA 1993b), concurrently with an exposure draft of a revised Code of Practice which was subsequently endorsed as a SORP by the ASB (CIPFA 1993a).

In summary, the proposals will radically affect a local authority's balance sheet and revenue accounts. Balance sheets will in future have to include fixed assets capitalised on an accruals basis, involving the compilation of asset registers, revalued quinquennially as a minimum. Operational assets, including land and buildings, are to be included at current value, defined as replacement cost, adjusted to reflect the condition of the existing asset, that is its "net current replacement cost". For certain assets, such as vehicles and equipment, depreciated historical cost may be shown as a proxy for current value. Infrastructure and community assets are to be shown at historical cost (this may be nil, and treated as a sunk cost). The book value of all fixed assets is to be written down annually by a provision for depreciation where applicable. However, when an authority can demonstrate that it is undertaking regular repairs and maintenance to extend the asset's useful life in its existing use, a depreciation provision need not be made.

Differences between revalued amounts and current net book values (which, for a local authority, is the historic cost less capital discharged, or the amount which has been repaid) are to be credited to a Fixed Asset Restatement Reserve. The balance on this reserve will reflect fluctuations over time in the aggregate value of an authority's fixed assets, including disposal of assets. The balance, of course, does not represent cash and is not available to finance expenditure. It is, in effect, an Inflation (or Revaluation) Reserve.

In future years, the accrued amount of capital expenditure must be reconciled with actual cash expenditure as this forms the basis of governmental control. The "excess" of expenditure will be accounted for by a decrease in working capital, that is an increase in capital creditors.

Two additional reserves are the Usable Capital Receipts Reserve (the same as the current capital receipts unapplied reserve), showing the amount available to finance future capital expenditure, and the Capital Financing Reserve, identified earlier.

With regard to revenue accounts, a system of asset rental accounting is to be adopted whereby revenue accounts incur a capital charge for all fixed assets used in the provision of the service. Such a charge must be at least equivalent to the annual provision for depreciation, if applicable, plus a notional interest charge to reflect the opportunity cost of the capital. However, these charges will not directly affect the local authority's "bottom line" nor, therefore, taxation decisions. The accounting entries are such that they are effectively replaced in the consolidated summary revenue account by the actual amounts of depreciation and interest payable. This is achieved by offsetting the debited amounts in individual service accounts with corresponding credits to an asset management revenue account, leaving the balance comprising depreciation and interest payable so that the capital charges are "reversed out" in the summary revenue account.

The restyled consolidated revenue account comprises four sections. The first itemises the cost of individual services, but because capital charges are now included there will be a significant increase in net expenditure, or "net cost of services", from that previously reported. Section two shows the component parts of the asset management revenue account and the balance on the account is added to the net cost of services to give "net operating expenditure". Section three shows all appropriations, or transfers to revenue or capital reserves. These appropriations are not expenditure and their "equivalent" would not be included in a company's profit and loss account. However, the requirement of the 1989 Act for a minimum revenue provision (MRP) for the payment of external loans means that, although the depreciation provision may be regarded as an MRP, this may be more or less than the amount required. Where the depreciation provision exceeds the statutory MRP, the revenue account will need to be credited with a sum equal to the excess; where the depreciation provision is less than the MRP it will need to be supplemented by an amount to be credited to a Capital Financing Reserve. The sum of the appropriations is added to the net operating expenditure to give "amount to be met from government grants and local taxation". The fourth section shows the principal sources of finance. This allows the "net surplus/deficit" to be shown (which is the net surplus/deficit on the general or county fund).

In considering the significance of the SORP, it needs to be remembered that capital accounting had to be adopted by most local authority Direct Service Organisations (DSOs) which provide services under Compulsory Competitive Tendering (CCT) and which have to achieve, on a current cost basis, a given rate of return on capital employed. The extension of CCT to white collar services necessitates closer analysis of overheads and use of assets.

However, an immediate requirement of the SORP was the compilation of asset registers, which in turn involved identification and valuation of assets. With regard to the central issue, the changes are meant to make local authority accounts meaningful, more comprehensible and comparable to best commercial practice. They should encourage more efficient use of resources. This was summarised by Evans (quoted in Jack 1993a) who stated: "If you don't have to pay for assets you are not going to worry about how you use them." They should also facilitate intra- and inter-authority comparisons of performance and efficiency, thereby enhancing managerial accountability (Darg 1993).

There are, however, counter-arguments (See Pipe 1993). The cost of implementing the new arrangements has been estimated by CIPFA to be £7m for Great Britain, with a recurring £1m per annum for revaluations, though it is conceded that "This estimate can only be the most general of indicators because it is based primarily on one authority's experience" (CIPFA 1993c) that is Solihull. Although this is a tiny sum when compared with total local authority expenditure, it is nonetheless an amount which could be used for other purposes and may represent a significant understatement.

With regard to asset registers, although the SORP does not require a definitive list of individual assets, nor a single register, it is nonetheless a potentially onerous exercise. The valuation of the assets is also problematic, and potentially dramatic. The pilot study at Solihull resulted in its fixed assets being revalued from £117m to £588m. However, although professional guidance will be sought, there is considerable scope for anomalies. Valuations, despite the adoption of standard professional techniques including standard formulae and banded land values, may result in inconsistencies across authorities. Similarly, authorities need not attribute values to assets which are deemed to be below a de minimis level, but the de minimis level is to be decided by each individual authority. In addition, the discretion allowed in respect of frequency of revaluations and the choice of specific asset valuation (historic or net replacement cost) will almost inevitably create inconsistencies. In turn, these will lead to fundamental anomalies with respect to capital charges (or asset rentals). Although they must at least cover a depreciation provision plus a capital financing charge, beyond that the SORP does not prescribe how they are to be determined or the basis of them.

The above points lead to legitimate reservations concerning the potential validity and usefulness of figures to be included in the published accounts. It is also taken as axiomatic that the new system of accounting will result in more efficient use of resources. This also will have to be monitored and ultimately substantiated.

Two final points must also be noted. Irrespective of a local authority's general policy on revaluation, DSO rate of return statements will still have to be produced on an annual basis and therefore require annual revaluation of assets used by the DSO. Second, it is important to note that the new arrangements do not include housing. This is clearly a significant omission, particularly for district councils and metropolitan authorities where housing will constitute the largest single element of an authority's assets. However, it was excluded because of perceived legal difficulties arising mainly from the requirements of the Local Government and Housing Act 1989.

Conclusion

It is recognised that public sector organisations in general and local authorities in particular are operating in a hostile and uncertain environment. The emphasis on commercialisation and market forces is something to which they must respond. However, public sector organisations, particularly central government, local government and the NHS, are not commercial organisations. In the main they provide services and, insofar as they must compete with the private sector and with each other (for example under CCT or the internal market in the NHS), the importance of charging for capital is unlikely to be significant.

This is not to argue that public sector resource accounting has no merit but rather it is to appreciate the simple point made by Henley (1992 p95) of central government but which applies to the public sector generally: "The questions always to be asked are: 'What purposes is the accounting treatment intended to serve?' and 'How will a particular presentation improve decision-taking?' not 'What are the professional accounting rules for this type of expenditure?', because they may or may not, in the public sector, be relevant." Rigid imitation of commercial practice may not always serve a useful purpose.

References

AHST (Association of Health Service Treasurers) (1985) *Managing Capital Assets in the National Health Service* London, CIPFA

CIPFA (1993a) *Code of Practice on Local Authority Accounting in Great Britain: A Statement of Recommended Practice* London CIPFA

CIPFA (1993b) *Capital Accounting by Local Authorities: report of the Capital Accounting Working Group* London CIPFA

CIPFA (1993c) "Institute Statement: Capital Accounting" *Public Finance and Accountancy* 19 Feb pp14–18

CIPFA (1987) *Code of Practice on Local Authority Accounting* London

CIPFA (1984) *Capital Accounting in Local Authorities – Second Report* London

CIPFA (1983) *Capital Accounting in Local Authorities* London

Cook, P. (1987) "Towards a Code of Practice on Local Authority Accounting – A New CIPFA/Audit Commission Consultation Paper" *Financial Accountability & Management* Vol 3 No 1 pp59–70

Coombs, H.M. and Edwards, J.R. (1992) "Capital Accounting in Municipal Corporations 1884–1914: Theory and Practice" *Financial Accountability & Management* Volume 8 No 3 pp181–201

Darg, A. (1993) "Improving asset management" *Public Finance and Accountancy* 9 July pp10–12

Davis, E. (1993) *The Importance of Resource Accounting* London, Social Market Foundation

DoE (1985) *Standardised Statements of Accounts for Local Authorities – Draft Regulations* London

Dept of Health (1989) *Working for Patients* London HMSO

Dixon, R. (1993) "Super-Charged NHS Hospitals" *Public Money & Management* Vol 13 No 3 pp57–60

Evans, M. (1993) "Fixed Assets revolution" *Accounting Technician* November pp44–45.

Henley, D. (1992) "Central Government" in Henley, D., Likierman, A., Perrin. J., Evans, M., Lapsley. I. and Whiteoak, J. *Public Sector Accounting and Financial Control* (4th Edition) London Chapman & Hall pp65–103

HMSO (1993) *Financial Statement and Budget Report 1994–5* London HMSO p93.

HMSO (1995) *Better accounting for the taxpayers' money* London HMSO

Jack, A. (1993a) "Local authorities called to account in an age of competitive tendering" *Financial Times* 25 February

Jones, G. (1996) "Resource Accounting and Budgeting: Another False Trail?" *Public Finance Foundation Review* No 10 pp7–9

Jones, R. (1985) "Accruals Accounting In UK Local Government: A Historical Context For Continuing Controversies" *Financial Accountability & Management* Vol 1 No 2, pp145–160

Jones, R. and Pendlebury, M. (1988) *Public Sector Accounting* (2nd Edition) London Pitman

Lapsley, I. (1986) "Managing Capital Assets In The National Health Service: A Critique" *Financial Accountability and Management* Vol 2 No 3 pp227–232

Likierman, A., Herald, D., Georgiou, G. and Wright, M. (1995) "Resource Accounting and Budgeting: A Symposium" *Public Administration* Vol 73 Winter pp561–570

Mayston, D. (1992a) "Capital Accounting, User Needs And The Foundations Of A Conceptual Framework For Public Sector Financial Reporting" *Financial Accountability & Management* Vol 8 No 4 pp247–248

Mayston, D. (1992b) "Financial Reporting In The Public Sector And The Demand For Information" *Financial Accountability & Management* Vol 8 No 4 pp317–324

Mellett, H. (1990) "Capital Accounting And Charges In The National Health Service After 1991" *Financial Accountability & Management* Vol 6 No 4 pp263–283

Mellett, H. (1988) "One Transplant the NHS Doesn't Need" *Accountancy* January pp118–119

Parkes, J. (1989) "Local Authority Capital Accounting – Towards Reform" *Financial Accountability & Management* Vol 5 No 2 pp107–118.

Perrin, J. (1992) "The National Health Service" in Henley, D. et al (1992)

Public Sector Accounting and Financial Control (4th Edition) London Chapman and Hall pp215–247

Pipe, J. (1993) "Capital accounting: the counter view" *Public Finance and Accountancy* 19 February pp20–21

8

Creative Accounting

David Neal

Introduction

Accounting, or more specifically financial reporting, is not a subject that lends itself to precision, and despite the claims of many of those involved in writing about and studying the subject area it can in no way claim to be scientific. Financial reporting will never be able to claim objectivity in the sense that many branches of science and engineering can. One example of the problems that this can cause is in the deep seated and much debated area of measurement in financial reports, which later we will show is a root of many of the issues which have collectively been called "creative accounting". A reporting accountant cannot measure the financial performance of a company in the same sense that an engineer can measure the tensile strength of a piece of steel since there are no undisputed measurement criteria available to an accountant whereas there are to the engineer. What makes it more difficult is that this problem may be incapable of resolution in accounting because some of the things the reporting accountant has to deal with are contingent on future events and as such can never be known with complete accuracy.

This requirement to report the future is the most clear cut of the measurement problems in accounting but is by no means the only one. Even events which can be regarded as complete in a temporal sense can be difficult to measure, an example of which is the whole area of cost allocation and costing methods. Thomas (1982) has characterised all allocations of cost as incorrigible and although his calls to end the process of cost allocation have been resisted by others on the grounds of pragmatism (Himmel, 1981; Liau 1981) they do not refute Thomas' fundamental point. In fact Himmel then counters showing that the alternative put forward by Thomas (cash flow reporting and a current value balance sheet) is in itself troubled by an "amalgamation" problem. This leads to different results depending on which level of amalgamation is chosen when there are no clear criteria for choosing one level over another.

This illustration of a specific problem in accounting also gives an indication of the problems involved in solving any dispute in accounting. The fact is that most issues in this area are debated in subjective terms since the objectives of financial reporting are themselves subjective. Terms such as relevance, reliability and representational faithfulness (ASB 1991) are all terms for which no unequivocal definition can be found and therefore their operational definition is likely to be the subject of continual debate and modification over time.

This may not be a bad thing since it can make for an interesting and lively subject area, and certainly for those in auditing practice it is the fact that judgement is involved, and the claim that the audit process also provides a public benefit, that enables them to claim the title of "profession" and with this charge professional levels of fees. The purely technical aspects of accounting, such as bookkeeping, do not have these (dubious?) advantages and services such as taxation advice must stand or fall solely on the economic benefit provided to the customer.

It is in the light of this continuing debate and the constant shift in understanding of the objectives of accounting that we shall examine the phenomena which have been grouped together under the title "creative accounting".

Creative Accounting – Definitions
We have seen above that accounting is not an exact science and that judgement must be used in a great many areas. In this sense then accounting is "naturally" creative and innovation should and will be a constant feature of the financial reporting environment. The preparer of accounts in presenting information will to some extent be faced by generic characteristics within the information and also by the unique context in which the events to be reported have occurred. If one were to give a large sample of accountants the same set of information about a reporting entity and asked them to prepare a set of financial statements under laboratory conditions then it is likely that there will be a large number of different outcomes for the

key components, such as profit after tax and net worth. If we were to take just one of these, such as profit, we would probably find that the outcomes were normally distributed about a mean profit figure. What we could not conclude from this hypothetical experiment is that the mean profit is in some way "superior" to the other fixtures; it is simply the most common occurrence.

What would change the outcome of this experiment is the existence of a regulator who has as his expressed aim the reduction in the variation of possible outcomes, that is in technical terms the reduction of the standard deviation of the outcomes. The amount of the reduction would depend largely on the regulator's view of the role of judgment within the financial reporting process.

If they were of the opinion that in order to produce a faithful representation of a company's affairs the preparer must be allowed some flexibility in the preparation of financial statements then the regulations are likely to allow different bases to be used for the same issue by different reporting entities. An alternative approach is that they are best served by choosing rigid criteria and enforcing compliance with these criteria, not withstanding whether the preparer thinks that this achieves a faithful representation of the entities' affairs. The difference between the two cases is whether the regulator favours representational faithfulness or comparability as the key goal of financial reports. In either case we would expect to see preparers innovate both around and beyond the extant regulation, and to "transform" the regulations to suit their own best interest. It is this innovation that has been most commonly given the title "creative accounting".

Creative accounting of this sort takes two principal forms which are, firstly where the innovation takes place in an area that is already the subject of regulation (for example the use of quasi subsidiaries to avoid the requirement to consolidate), and secondly where it covers an unregulated subject (for example the inclusion of brands in the balance sheet). It is to both types of innovation that we will ascribe the title creative accounting. It is important however to make a distinction between innovation in financial reporting and the use of accounting tools to hide illegal business activities, namely fraud. The raiding of the Mirror Group pension fund by Robert Maxwell certainly involved some innovative accounting but it was also clearly illegal; on this point there should be a clear distinction. The case of the Brent Walker Group does however illustrate that this boundary between fraud and creative accounting, in this case the "persuasive" use of accounting data, is not always clearly understood (at least not by the UK

Serious Fraud Office who brought the prosecution against George Walker, the founder and former CEO of the group).

To summarise we can break down creative accounting into four classes.

1. The creativity that is a "natural" element of financial reporting and is needed for representational faithfulness in reports. An example of this would be the available choice of depreciation methods.
2. The avoidance of the spirit of an accounting regulation by the development of an innovative accounting technique. An example of this would be the use of quasi subsidiaries.
3. The inclusion in financial reports of an item that is unregulated and which involves significant innovation. An example of this is the inclusion of brand names.
4. Fraud.   *David Neal*.

The definition of "creative accounting" that we will be using is based on only the second and third categories, and critically is dependent on the existence of a regulator. We shall therefore look next at the arguments surrounding the existence of accounting regulation.

The Regulation of Financial Reporting

The question "why regulate financial reporting" is considered by some (Naser 1993) to be the most controversial issue among accounting researchers. This statement itself may be said to be controversial but it is certainly an area where much has been written and a broad range of opinions put forward. The main area of debate is over the adequacy of market mechanisms, both in the market for financial information and in the arrangement of contracts between principal and agent (which include a reporting element) to provide adequate financial reporting. There is also the claim that the "constituency" of financial reporting includes the whole of society and that financial reporting and auditing play an important role in protecting the "public interest". One thing that becomes clear is that some agreement on the fundamental role of accounting would make the debate on regulation less contentious since there would be a benchmark against which to test the success or failure of the regulated or non-regulated environment. The lack of such a benchmark is evident from my earlier chapter in this volume on accounting theory.

The main arguments against regulation are those surrounding agency theory and the failure of accounting regulation to achieve adequate corporate governance. The second of these may be recast as a pro-regulation argument because its emphasis is on the failure of the current regime of regulation rather than all regimes of regulation for all time.

Agency theory involves analysing the relationship between the principal and the agent (shareholder and manager in this model) where ownership and control of assets is separated. The purpose of an agency contract is that the agent will act on behalf of the owner in return for which the agent will receive a fee or some other form of recompense, often related to the agent's performance in achieving some specified objective. The example of a theatrical agent who charged a percentage of the performers fee would be such a relationship. The premiss in the accounting literature is that there is a conflict of interest between owner and manager since their utility functions are unlikely to coincide. An example of this is where a manager will seek to diversify the activities of a company to reduce the risk of cyclical changes in income and to increase their own power base when this does not serve the interest of the shareholder because they could diversify much more simply and at less cost by trading in securities. The existence of this potential conflict means that contracts of this sort invariably have monitoring arrangements built in by the principal to control the behaviour of the agent and that these may involve significant cost.

The opponents of regulation argue that both agent and principal have sufficient incentive to make these monitoring arrangements work efficiently in the absence of regulation, based on the idea of an "efficient" market in the firm's securities. The argument can also be made that regulation by an outside body may be unsuitable for the needs of both parties to this "private contract" and will therefore add significantly to the cost of reporting, thereby encouraging evasion of regulation by both parties.

However there is an added complication in these monitoring arrangements, that of inequality of information between owner and manager. It is this inequality that some believe led to regulation in accounting as owners of capital required the intervention of government to protect their property interest (Tinker 1985). The proponents of agency theory argue however that this asymmetry will cause the owner to use incentive-based reward schemes, such as stock options, to equate the manager's utility to that of the owner.

Incentive-based reward schemes are inherently more risky to managers and therefore they will react by agreeing to restrictions on their behaviour, including for example a voluntary audit, to reduce agency costs. The result will be the required level of financial reporting at the minimum cost for both parties. A problem with this argument however is that it does not take into account the difficulties that the principal may have in arranging an efficient incentive contract. The problem here is related to the disposition of shareholdings. In most cases shares are held by a large number of disparate groups and individuals and therefore they do not find it easy to "negotiate" with a management proposal. This "asymmetry of organisation" tends to lead to incentive schemes that have many incentives but very few, if any, disincentives and too loose monitoring arrangements. An example of this is the explosion in remuneration for managers in the newly privatised utilities in the UK where managers awarded themselves hundreds of millions of pounds worth of share options with no significant change in the "effort" they were expected to produce. The difference can be accounted for by the fact that instead of dealing with a single principal (government) they are now dealing with a multiple owner who is less able or willing to scrutinise management action.

Proponents of regulations argue that even if the agency argument was not flawed, there is also a public good argument that precludes reliance on private contracts to control firms' behaviour. Information asymmetry between the firm and the "public" may lead to a redistribution of income that would be socially and politically unacceptable (Cooper and Schener 1984).

The other main argument against accounting regulation is that it fails to achieve an improvement in corporate governance. Benston (1982) uses the argument that it is impossible to tell whether a standard has a positive effect on corporate governance because there are no reliable measurement criteria. This leads to the argument that standard setting is not based on technical requirements but on political processes, and in the same way that managers maximise their own utility so too will those with influence over the political process of regulation. The standards produced will therefore not be the socially desirable ones but will be those that enhance the status quo and best defend the interest of those with power in the regulatory process, in particular the regulator itself. This may not be a call for an end to regulation but a call for the explicit acknowledgement of the political and a critical perspective on the supposed neutrality of the accounting profession.

Those who argue in favour of regulation have one main justification for doing so, that of market failure. This failure can be at two levels, firstly that of the failure to achieve an optimal distribution of resources between competing alternative investments because of inadequate or misleading information disclosure and secondly, even if there were efficient allocation of resources in the market, there is the issue of social choice in these issues particularly with regard to equity within markets and the distribution effects of accounting information. The classic dilemma of relying on the market is that of the "free-loader". Individually managers would do best to present their company in the best possible light, if necessary by the use of creative accounting practices. Collectively however it is better for the operation of the market, and therefore of all those concerned in it, to behave in a responsible manner and not seek to divert resources to inefficient investments. The problem is who is going to be the first one to start and how to deal with individuals who say that while they appreciate everybody else's bonhomie they are quite happy to maximise their own welfare on this occasion. The effect of this is that nobody would rationally behave in such a way to maximise total utility, instead they will maximise their own utility. The sum of the individual utility will therefore be sub-optimal for the group encouraging the entry of the regulator to govern behaviour and also to threaten punishment on those who exhibit this particular form of selfishness. This can be justified by the increased total utility. If the "disease" of free-loading could be resolved some other way then the argument for regulation would diminish on market grounds. The temptation for governments to intervene would still be strong on social and political grounds.

In conclusion, whether or not the arguments for or against regulation are persuasive, the fact of the matter is that accounting in most countries takes place in a regulated environment and that it appears to me that whatever the form of regulation, be it private sector or public sector, or some combination of the two, the instinct for self-preservation by the regulator and the political risk of de-regulation will ensure that accounting standards and accounting standard setters will survive.

Impact of Creative Accounting on Standard Setters

One of the reasons that creative accounting of the type described earlier has become such a big issue is that it causes acute embarrassment for the standard setting agency and acts to highlight ongoing unresolved debates surrounding some very basic and fundamental areas of disagreement. This may be seen as a sign of weakness on the part of the regulator.

There is, as discussed earlier, a natural and healthy degree of innovation in financial reporting, but some of the latest techniques are very disconcerting for standard setters because they run contrary to their stated aims of reducing divergence in accounting practice. In addition to this the gathering pace of innovation particularly in the field of financial instruments has put severe strain on the ability of the regulatory bodies to respond in a timely manner. In the case of the regulator in the UK, the failure to respond effectively led to its demise, or transformation, into a new and more highly resourced body. The jury is still deliberating on whether this was a success or not.

Many of the developments that have threatened the standard setting process have not been for the purpose of creating accounting illusions but have been caused by attempts to achieve more efficient funding of business activities. An example of this is the growing use of derivatives, which are not merely an illusion created for accounting purposes but innovative attempts to redistribute risks and rewards. However some tools have been developed with no other end than to achieve an accounting result. An example of this is deliberate splitting of a transaction into a series of separate transactions so that when accounted for separately, as opposed to together, the result is different. This was defined by ED42 as a special purpose transaction. The use of options is common in this type of arrangement. An example of this is where a whisky distiller "sells" his stock of maturing whisky to a bank with an option for the bank to "put" it back to the distiller at some time in the future for an agreed price and an equal and opposite option for the distiller to "call" it back at that same price. The price is set at cost plus an interest charge. The option is certain to be exercised in this case by one party or the other. The accounting treatment if it were a separate series of transactions would be a sale (with related profit recorded in the accounts) and then a separate purchase of stock in the future. If accounted for in the manner suggested in ED42, as a series of linked transactions, then the substance of this series is that of a mortgage loan secured against stock, which is undoubtabley the "truth" of the matter, as the bank has no intention of entering the whisky trade!

This type of transaction is based on a crucial pair of assumptions. The first is that the auditor of the financial statements is unable to draw sufficient attention to the creative accounting tool. This can be in terms of not being able to discover the transaction in the first instance because of the sampling error in the audit process or, perhaps even more critically, they are constrained by their relationship with the companies' management from either forcing a change in the financial reports or from qualifying their audit report to highlight the problem to potential readers of the accounts.

The independence or otherwise of the auditor and the potential solutions to both of the above problems are beyond the scope of this chapter, but two points should be made. The first is that auditors find it easier to impose an accounting treatment on reluctant managers if it is supported by regulation rather than if it is a question of judgment. The auditor of a company that insisted on capitalising brand names and then refused to depreciate those brands would find it much easier to resist client pressure to do this if there were a definitive standard that outlined acceptable brand valuation cases and insisted that they be amortised over a set period. This may not be the perfect solution to brand accounting but it would strengthen the auditor's hand, and reduce the third type of creative accounting outlined above. The problem is that the pace of innovation has outstripped the pace of regulation and also that regulation is reactive rather than proactive in these instances.

The second assumption that is crucial to understanding creative accounting is that users of accounts allow themselves, or are believed to allow themselves, to be deceived by cosmetic accounting devices. The latter belief is reinforced by the "*apparently* excessive weight given by financial analysis to 'bottom line' earnings figures and gearing ratios" (Tweedie and Whittington 1990 p97)[emphasis added]. This runs contrary to most opinion in the finance literature which characterises capital markets in both the UK and the US as semi-strong efficient. One conclusion from this is that most of the people putting the effort into creative accounting have not read this literature or if they have read it then they did not understand it, since one of the consequences of efficiency in capital markets is that there is "no such thing as an accounting illusion". The other conclusion from the existence of creative accounting is that the finance literature is wrong, which would bring the house of cards down on most of this area of study.

Accounting standard setters also seem to follow this theory of the naive user, as illustrated by the publicity surrounding FRS3 where the head of the ASB, Tweedie himself, urged people to use a range of performance indicators and not simply the EPS ratio. This urging assumes that users were only using EPS, for which no evidence was produced. People such as Terry Smith (1992), who is himself an analyst, perpetuate this myth. Intuitively one can feel little sympathy for a highly-paid analyst who advised his banking employer to invest in a client and then claims that he (among others) was fooled by a relatively simple accounting device.

The general public (whoever they might be) could make such an excuse but being aware of their weakness they enter the market for information at great cost and purchase the services of said Mr Smith. To add insult to injury you can then publish an exposé of inadequacies and make a substantial profit from it (Smith 1992). Nice work if you can get it, and proof indeed that there is indeed a "market for excuses" (Watts and Zimmerman 1979).

The perception of the role of the regulator, the role of the auditor and the gullibility of the users of financial statements are all vital constituent parts when asking why preparers put time and effort into creative accounting. If we fall back on the fundamental assumptions of agency theory of individuals maximising their own utility (an assumption shared with much of micro economics) and that they see no benefit in behaving altruistically (in the public interest at their own cost), then they must be doing so for some perceived benefit. This benefit can only be achieved if the regulator is unable to stop or publicise the creative tool before some benefit can be obtained.

The importance of publicity is that it gives the game away to some extent and therefore in most, but not all, cases it thwarts the objectives of creative accounting. The decision by Rank Hovis McDougall plc (RHM) to capitalise "home grown" brand valuations in their balance sheet, is an interesting case in point. The decision to capitalise brands was met by a typical reactive exposure draft produced by the ASC (ED52 Accounting for Intangible Fixed Assets).

This permitted the capitalisation of "acquired" brands where they were distinguishable from other goodwill as long as they were amortised in the same way as that suggested by ED47 Accounting for Goodwill. But if home grown brands were treated in the same way as home grown goodwill then it is not permitted to include these in the balance sheet. RHM proceeded to capitalise home grown brands to the tune of £688m despite the obvious similarity to home grown goodwill. They were not technically in breach of a regulation but they were certainly in breach of the spirit of the regulator's thinking at the time. The capitalisation did not go unpublicised but in this case, publicity was in fact one of the desired effects of the management of RHM in pursuing this policy since one of their objectives was to highlight what they perceived was an undervaluation of the company by the market in the light of a hostile takeover bid. Other cases of creative accounting, such as some complex group arrangements, might depend on non-discovery for success. The regulator has still not responded in a definitive way to the brand capitalisation issue and RHM continue to hold home made brands in their balance sheet. To rub salt into the wounds they also do not provide any depreciation against these brands.

The position of the auditor in this case is clear in that at no time did RHM receive a qualified audit report, indicating approval of the treatment of brands by the auditor. This is interesting as the audit profession is heavily involved in the standard setting process in the UK and uses compliance with accounting regulations as part of the necessary conditions for arriving at a "true and fair view" on the reports. The role of the auditor in supporting the RHM cause is even more evident in their support of non-depreciation, since this involves invocation of the so called "true and fair override", since without this non-depreciation is contrary to UK statute. The use of this override requires more than tacit acceptance by the auditor since a valid explanation for its use must be given in the notes to the accounts.

The position of the users of the RHM reports is far harder to ascertain since by the general consensus of many regulators (FASB, ASB, IASC, etc.) the user group consists of most of the population in one guise or another, and it would be impossible to ask each of them individually what impact it had on them. Equally a market reaction study would be difficult since it would be impossible to separate the effect of the brand valuation from any other effect on share price in and individual case.

Further Examples of Creative Accounting
The use of creative techniques can be divided in a number of ways but most types of creative accounting can be classified into one of three groups.

1. The "creation" of new assets to enhance the appearance of the balance sheet. Examples of this are accounting for intangible fixed assets and capitalisation of interest in the construction of fixed assets.
2. The removal of an asset and its related liability from the balance sheet, again to improve its appearance. Examples of this are sale and leaseback schemes, use of unincorporated or non-controlled subsidiaries, and the use of consignment stock.
3. Techniques that seek to "massage" reported earnings. Examples of this are the allocation of fair values on the acquisition of a subsidiary, accounting for reorganisation costs, gains from the sale of fixed assets and complex capital arrangements such as deep discounted bonds and stepped interest bonds.

Space precludes an exhaustive account of each of these techniques (Table 1 contains examples of some specific cases of creative accounting) so we will be looking primarily at the motivation of the preparer in using the techniques and the common threads that link them. In doing this we will follow the model developed by Tweedie and Whittington (1990), which identifies two common strands to creative accounting techniques and within those strands two further classifications. The two strands are measurement problems, which sub-divides into valuation and capital maintenance; and recognition problems which sub-divides into boundaries of the group entity and definitions of assets and liabilities. The generic problems of measurement and recognition appear to be intractable and have resulted in draft chapters in a "Statements of Principle" (ASB 1992) rather than a definitive solution.

An important point to consider in the use of the Tweedie and Whittington model is that, with regard to the desired effect of the creative technique, there is no analysis of the motivation of the preparer in using the technique or whether the desired effect is actually achieved if it is employed. Fundamental questions as to the real value of financial reports and the reaction of capital markets to creative accounting techniques remain unanswered. Because the difficulty in measuring the benefit in adopting a creative accounting technique affects all the parties involved in accounting (preparers, regulators and academics) we have to assume that preparers perceive that benefit accrues to them, or at least that the preparer is willing to bear the cost of the use of the creative technique on the chance that benefit will follow its use.

From the perspective of the regulator it is more straightforward since there is no benefit, only a potential threat to his authority. Given that this threat is to his very existence, the regulator is bound to take the issue with a great deal of seriousness. To some extent at least, the establishment of the "real" effect becomes a side issue. The perception that there could be some methods which might mislead users is enough to stir both sides into action (or more accurately to make the preparers act and the regulator react).

Where the Tweedie and Whittington approach is useful is in identifying the clear themes that run through the issues collectively known as creative accounting. These clear themes are recognition problems and measurement problems.

Recognition problems involve when and whether to include an economic event or series of events in the financial statements. This can be narrowed down further into the problems of defining the boundaries of the reporting entity and then the problem of defining such terms as asset, liability and other components of the accounts. The definitions would be sufficiently clear to decide which category an item would be placed in even when faced with the most complex of transactions. Such definitions do not currently exist. The seemingly intractable problem of producing such definitions is that classification is often contingent on the outcome of some future event.

Measurement problems are also affected by the uncertainty over future outcomes. The two central issues relating to measurement are valuation and capital maintenance. These two issues are interlinked in that the choice of valuation technique for inclusion of assets in the balance sheet will usually determine the capital maintenance concept to be used when determining how much of the "surplus" from the firm's activities should go to shareholders and how much should be withheld to maintain capital. So historic cost in the balance sheet implies historic cost capital maintenance, and replacement cost (or entry value) implies a replacement cost (or physical

TABLE 1.

	Desired Effect	Loopholes Used	Accounting Problems	Possible Solutions	Response
Off Balance Sheet Schemes					
1. Operating and Finance Leases	Reduction of gearing	b	Loose definition	Tighter definitions or emphasis on truth and fairness	FRS 5 Tighter definitions and examples given
2. Controlled non-subsidiaries	Removal of assets and liabilities from group accounts	a	Legal definitions out of date/ loose definition in accounting standard	Redefinition of subsidiary (CA89&ED49)	FRS 2 - Subsidiary Redefined
3. Contingent Contracts	Removal of assets and liabilities from balance sheet	b	Lack of definition of assets/ Liabilities	Redefinition of assets/liabilities	FRS 5 - Partial coverage
Business Combinations					
4. Merger and acquisition accounting	Control of (i) profit for the year of combination and following years (ii) gearing ratios	c & d	Two treatments dealing with similar events	One treatment	FRS 6
5. Fair Value	Avoidance of increased depreciation or improvement of gearing	c & d	Two treatments dealing with similar events	One treatment,; one valuation system	FRS 7
6. Reorganisation Expenses	Increased income	c & d	Two treatments for similar situations	One treatment, can no longer be included in acquisition costs and goodwill calculation	FRS 7
7. Goodwill/Brand Accounting	1. Avoidance of annual amortisation 2. Increase or reduction of gearing ratios	b, c & d	Two treatments for similar situation	One treatment, based on a consistent definition of intangible asset	Discussion document only
8. Equity Issues	Increased profits	a	Is retained profit attributable to the group?	Recognition only if cash retained in associate company is accessible	Discussion document only
Complex capital Issues					
9. Various	1. Increase profit (by reducing interest charge) 2. Reducing gearing	b, c & d	1. Profit does not reflect full interest charge 2. Gearing ratio distorted	1. Accrue full interest charge 2. Redefine equity, borrowing, minority interest 3. Develop rule on treatment of uncertainty of conversion	FRS 4
10. Irregular Valuations	1. Higher income because depreciation charges low if revaluation delayed 2. Gains on disposal greater if revaluation delayed 3. Gearing ratio reduced if revaluation undertaken	c & d	No rule for regular revaluation	Requirement for regular revaluation	FRS 3 Suggest revaluation but does not make it mandatory

Source: Tweedie & Whittington (1990)

Key to Table One

Recognition
Boundaries of Group Entity   a
Definition of Assets, Equity, Liabilities, etc.   b
Measurement
Valuation   c
Capital Maintenance   d

capacity) capital maintenance concept. The debate over the merits of different valuation techniques is deep seated in the accounting literature, with a wide range of opinions as to the "best" technique. The only conclusion from this debate is that no single method of valuation will be appropriate for all circumstances, but recent reports (McMonnies 1988 and Solomans 1989) on the future direction of financial reporting in the UK agree that some form of current market value should be the basis of financial reporting practice. What is unclear is whether this would lead to the demise of creative accounting or its expansion. The solution of some current problems, such as merger versus acquisition accounting, would lead to their replacement by other problems mainly involving the use of judgment in the valuation of assets which is inherent to any current value regime.

Conclusion

A solution to the problems of measurement and valuation would greatly assist in a solution to the current set of issues collectively known as creative accounting. However given the nature of any solution to either problem it is likely that current problems will be replaced by a new one. The conclusion that must therefore be drawn is that creative accounting is in fact an inherent part of accounting and is something that simply goes with the job if you take on the role of regulator. Therefore the reactive rather than proactive position of the regulator is likely to continue. Tweedie and Whittington conclude that the area which would benefit most from research is the area of uncertainty. It could be argued that better disclosure of the nature of the events that lead to uncertainty in either measurement or recognition could improve the information content of accounts. The fundamental issue of uncertainty is however incapable of resolution.

The other issue that could lead to the belief that creative accounting is a permanent phenomenon is the constant innovation of firms with regard to financial structure and the move away from the creation of physical assets towards knowledge-based assets. The regulator cannot be expected to be proactive since the innovation cannot be anticipated. There are going to continue to be "new products" in financial reporting which are unregulated and therefore give scope for creativity. For these reasons a similar review of creative accounting will be equally valid in ten years time. Although the detailed content may change the phenomenon of creative accounting is here to stay.

References

Accounting Standards Board (1991 a) Exposure Draft "Foreward to Accounting Standards" *Accountancy* September pp 104–105

Accounting Standards Board (1991 b) Exposure Draft – Statement of Principles "The Objective of Financial Statements and the Qualitative Characteristics of Financial Information" *Accountancy* September pp 99–103

Arnold, J. and Hope, A. (1975) "Reporting Business Performance" *Accounting and Business Research* Spring pp 96–105

ASC (1988), ED42 *Accounting for special purpose transactions*

ASC (1990) ED47 *Accounting for Goodwill*

ASC (1990) ED49 *Reflecting the substance of transactions in assets and liabilities*

ASC (1990) ED52 *Accounting for intangible fixed assets*

Belkaoui, A.R. (1992) *Accounting Theory* Third Edition London Academic Press

Benston, E.J. (1982) "Accounting and Corporate Accountability" *Accounting Organisations and Society* 7 pp87–105

Cooper, D.J. and Sherer, M.J. (1984) "The Value of Corporate Accounting Reports: Arguments for a Political Economy of Accounting" *Accounting Organisations and Society* September pp 207–32

Dopuch, N. and Sunder, S. (1980) "FASB's Statements on Objectives and Elements of Financial Accounting: A Review" *The Accounting Review* January pp 1–19

Financial Reporting Council (1992) *Second Annual Review – The State of Financial Reporting* London Financial Reporting Council

Griffiths, I. (1987) *Creative Accounting* London, Unwin

Himmel, S. (1981) "Financial Allocations Justified" *CA Magazine* October pp 70–73

Horngren, C.T. (1972) "Accounting Principles; Private or Public Sector" *Journal of Accountancy* May pp37–41

Jones, M. (1989) "Stimulation or Revolution" *Accountancy* April pp 106–108

Naser, K.H.M. (1993) *Creative Financial Accounting* Hemel Hempstead Prentice Hall

McMonnies, P. (ed) (1988) *Making corporate reports more valuable* Edinburgh and London ICAS and Kogan Page

Smith, T. (1992) *Accounting for Growth* London, Century

Solomans, D. (1978) "The politicisation of accounting" *Journal of Accountancy* November pp65–72

Solomans, D. (1989) *Guidelines for financial reporting standards* London ICAEW

Solomans, D. (1991) "Accounting and Social Change : A Neutralist View" *Accounting, Organisations and Society* vol 16 no3 pp287–295

Sterling, R.R. (1970) "On Theory Construction and Verification" *Accounting Review* July pp444–457

Thomas, A.L. (1982) "Why Financial Allocations Can't be Justified" *CA Magazine* April pp 28–31

Tweedie, D. (1983) Review of "A Conceptual Framework for Financial Accounting and Reporting" *Accounting and Business Research* Summer pp 238–239

Tweedie, D. and Whittington, G. (1990) "Financial Reporting: Current problems and their implications for systematic reform" *Accounting and Business Research* vol21 no81 pp87–102

Watts, R. and Zimmerman, J. (1978) "Towards a positive theory of the determination of accounting standards" *Accounting Review* January pp112–134

Watts, R. and Zimmerman, J. (1979) "The demand and supply of accounting theories: a market for excuses" *The Accounting Review* February pp273–305

Woolf, E. (1990) "That Elusive Conceptual Framework" *Accountancy* February pp63–64

9

Insolvency and the Role of the Accountant

Jennifer Lane Lee

Introduction

Between 1986, when the new Insolvency Act was introduced, and 1993, nearly 173,000 companies went through the insolvency system (Insolvency Executive Agency). The scale of the failures, and the apparent failure of the new system to ease the burdens of troubled companies has led to a growing call for reform. One aspect of the operation of the Act which has attracted particular critical attention is the perceived lack of accountability of the accountants and practitioners who serve the system.

Accountancy is a profession which, like the legal profession, is quite technical in nature. This technical orientation contrasts sharply with the practical, creative orientation of business. These distinct approaches seldom come into conflict in the day-to-day conduct of business, but in the instances where accountancy becomes involved in the realm of insolvency, the ordinarily peaceful coexistence sometimes dissolves. Thus, of the 3,420 complaints received by the professional conduct department of the Institute of Chartered Accountants in England and Wales (ICAEW) in 1992, 13 per cent of them related to insolvency matters (Jack 7 June 1994).

This chapter will explore some of the controversy currently surrounding the role of the accountant in the implementation of the UK insolvency system. It will begin with a brief exploration of the technical side of insolvency, including a look at the operation of the insolvency system. This overview will be followed by a closer examination of the role the accountant plays in the system and a discussion of how this role may conflict with the approach of a troubled firm as well as with the accountant's own ethical codes of practice.

By way of illustration, a case study will explore the power an accounting firm may legitimately wield, and the conflict of interest which may arise. This case study will serve to introduce the discussion of the professional and ethical obligations of the insolvency practitioner.

When a Firm Becomes Insolvent

Insolvency occurs, under the Insolvency Act (IA) of 1986, when a firm is unable to pay its debts. To determine when a company has become "unable to pay its debts," accountants rely on one of two tests: the "commercial" test and the "balance sheet" test (Jones 1993).

The commercial test [IA s123(1)(a)(b)] is the most common test used to justify a winding up order (Jones 1993 p133). According to this test, a company is deemed insolvent where (a) a creditor who is owed more than £750 has served a written demand upon the company and that demand has not been paid for three weeks; or (b) if any execution or process issued on judgment decree or order of the court is not satisfied in whole or in part.

The second test, the balance sheet test, assesses the value of the company's assets relative to its liabilities. If the assets are less than the liabilities (including contingent and prospective liabilities), then the firm is deemed to be insolvent according to the balance sheet test. This test is most important in the instigation of the insolvency procedure known as administration (see below) and in assessing the conduct of management prior to insolvency.

The question of solvency or insolvency is generally resolved by an accountant. Often, the accountant is serving in the capacity of an investigative accountant appointed by a creditor which is concerned about its security. Where an accountant determines that the firm is insolvent, the tenets of the Insolvency Act 1986 and/or the Companies Act 1985 come into play.

The Aims and Objectives of the Insolvency System

Current insolvency laws exist to prevent a destructive race on a company's assets. Put another way, the philosophical aim of insolvency law is to regulate the pursuit of claims so as to prevent the "free for all ... of individual claims by different creditors. ..." and replace it with a mechanism that allows for the collection and realisation of assets and their equitable distribution amongst individual claimants (Goode 1990 p2). Prior to 1986, the law favoured creditors in the distribution of assets. It also focused on the punishment of debtors. In 1976, after years of complaints about the insolvency system, the government established a committee under the chairmanship of Sir Kenneth Cork to reappraise the entire insolvency system. The "Cork Committee" (1980) advised that the time had come for a new law governing insolvency and criticised the law's predilection for "retributive and punitive justice toward the debtor." It recommended that the balance of the system be tilted away from punishment and toward rehabilitation. Today, the revised UK insolvency law is based on the Insolvency Act of 1986 (and corresponding Insolvency Rules), and the Companies Act of 1985.

The specific objectives of the current law can be inferred from the powers granted to creditors or to the Official Receiver acting on behalf of the creditors. The first noted objective is to remove directors from management. It is a long-standing principle of UK law that those in power when a company fails should have no significant continuing management role (Goode 1990 p6). Moreover, directors who have been determined unfit to manage should be punished for losses caused to creditors and employees (Goode 1990 p8). The Department of Trade and Industry is charged with investigating the causes of company failure and punishing culpable directors and officers.

The second objective is to suspend individual actions by creditors, so as to prevent the destructive "free for all." In order to prevent a free for all, the insolvency system attempts to ensure an orderly and fair ranking of creditors and a distribution of assets reflecting that ranking. The system as formulated today involves the establishment of a queue that competing creditors must accept. Secured creditors and debenture holders with floating charges are first in the queue, followed by preferred creditors, those with claims arising from the insolvency proceedings (most notably the insolvency practitioners acting as receivers or liquidators) and redundant employees. However, there are special cases in all forms of insolvency wherein certain classes of claimant's individual rights are not affected. For instance, an unsecured creditor can put a company which is already in administrative receivership into liquidation over the objections of other creditors (Sealy and Milman 1988 373).

To ensure a fair ranking and distribution of assets, the third objective of the system is to prevent or void transactions which are deemed to be unfair to creditors. Should a director allow a trade while the company is insolvent or should an insolvency practitioner diminish the value of a company through trade, they can be pursued for damages by creditors and the former practitioner can be disqualified (Griffiths and Williams 1986 pp5–14).

The fourth objective of the system established in the 1986 Act is to facilitate the recovery of companies. Insolvency practitioners are instructed to seek the best possible outcome for creditors. This may mean that a company in receivership or administration can trade out of insolvency (Cork Gully (A) 2). Unfortunately, this last objective often stumbles before Britain's apparent lack of a "rescue culture." The insolvency system has a stated interest in preserving assets and jobs wherever possible. Nevertheless, as Christopher Morriss (1994 p43) explains, "The UK understanding of 'rescue' has always been based on the notion that there is no public interest in preserving insolvent corporate shells and their stakeholders; in other words, the phrase 'risk capital' means precisely what it says."

The painful issue nevertheless remains of how the system can strike a balance between dismantling firms that are well and truly dying or dead and preserving those that still have a hope of fruitful existence.

The Insolvency Procedures

The variety of insolvency procedures are revealed in the Insolvency [IA 1986] and Companies Acts [CA 1985]. These procedures include: voluntary arrangements, administration, administrative receivership and liquidation. Liquidations can either be compulsory or voluntary.

Administration, one of the major innovations of the 1986 Act, has often been described as the UK equivalent of America's Chapter 11 provision. It is instituted through an application to the Court for an administrative order installing an insolvency practitioner as company administrator. The petition must be supported by the affidavits of the company, its director, and/or its creditors. These affidavits must declare that it is unlikely that the company will be able to repay its debts. They must also state the objectives in invoking the procedure, the company's financial position, the details of any ongoing legal proceedings pending and, finally, the firm's belief that it has complied with Rule 2.2 which requires an in-depth, independent report on the company's affairs.

Administration orders may be granted when one or more of the following outcomes is likely to be achieved (County NatWest WoodMac 1991 31):

(a) the survival of all or part of the company;

(b) the approval by creditors of a voluntary arrangement to restructure the company;

(c) the sanctioning of a compromise or other revised arrangement between creditors and the company (such as a CA s425 voluntary arrangement);

(d) a more advantageous realisation of the assets of a company than a winding up.

Once an administrator is appointed, the appointment of a receiver or the enforcement of security claims against company assets is not allowed.

The administration procedure, while one of the primary innovations of the 1986 Act, has not lived up to expectations and is rarely put into practice (see Table 1). The reasons for its failure are many.

First, the procedure is subservient to the receivership procedure. That is, secured creditors can veto a request for an administration procedure and instead appoint their own receiver. Moreover, secured creditors, usually banks, will rarely agree to an administration procedure because, as a court-based procedure, it is very complex and often costly relative to other procedures. For instance, the Rule 2.2 requirement on its own can be very expensive and time-consuming to complete.

Another problem with administration is the fact that the procedure cannot stand alone; it must be followed by a Company Voluntary Arrangement (see below for a discussion of CVAs) or a Companies Act scheme, if restructuring is to occur. Moreover, the board of directors is automatically replaced by the administrator, removing potentially valuable experience and making directors reluctant to initiate the procedure themselves.

Finally, administration is not very amenable to small firms. Secured creditors such as banks will generally veto administration, especially for small firms where the prospective costs of the procedure could outweigh the value of the bank's security. Also, as noted above, the company must comply with Insolvency Rule 2.2 which requires an in-depth, independent report on the company' affairs. This is generally beyond the financial capacity of most small, troubled firms.

After a lengthy discussion period, the DTI has recently recommended a simplified version of the administration procedure be implemented along with a 28-day moratorium. Whether these alterations actually become law and, more importantly, whether they satisfy the problems inherent in the current procedure remains to be seen.

Company voluntary arrangements (CVA) are arrangements made between the company and its creditors without recourse to the formal insolvency system (CA 1985 s425). This procedure is usually recommended where the company has suffered short-term problems that can potentially be remedied. Because of the costs, the expanded time scales, the varying positions of debtors and creditors, and the inability to obtain a protective interim order, this technique has rarely been used by companies (Insolvency Bulletin 1992 p7; *Economist* 1992). Under a CVA, the company is completely exposed until the Court sanctions the scheme, so a creditor can call in the receiver over the heads of other creditors whenever it thinks its interests are prejudiced. Also, the CVA offers no protection to the company director from prosecution for wrongful trading should the company continue trading.

All this leaves the insolvent company in a very precarious position and, as a result, the procedure is at present only used at the end of an administration order when an insolvent firm is well on the road to recovery (Jack 1993).

Administrative receivership, the most common recovery procedure, occurs when a creditor (usually a bank) is unwilling to continue supporting a company and asks the board of directors to invite it to appoint insolvency practitioners to act as administrative receivers. In most cases a bank has decided to collect on its floating charge. The normal outcome is the sale of all or part of the business with the proceeds put towards the repayment of the outstanding debts. Creditors get paid in full in order of seniority until the money runs out.

Administrative receivership is less expensive than administration since it avoids court involvement, but it allows for no restructuring of debt. It also means the end of involvement in the company for its directors. However, in this respect, it is less onerous than liquidation as there is less likelihood of them being investigated and declared unfit to act as directors in the future.

Liquidation, the final option for insolvent companies, is relatively straight-forward process. Liquidation can be either voluntary, where shareholders appoint a liquidator and ask creditors to approve their action, or it can be compulsory, where a creditor applies to the Court for referral to the Official Receiver. The Official Receiver in a compulsory liquidation can either appoint a liquidator or can act in that capacity himself.

Liquidation is a last resort action. There is little chance that any but the most senior creditors will receive full recompense. The Official Receiver or appointed liquidator is there to dispose of assets as quickly and as efficiently as possible. Liquidations always involve an investigation into the conduct of the directors and can lead to their disqualification from holding any management role for from two to 15 years. (Cork Gully Directors (B) 2).

Department of Trade and Industry statistics, covering all sizes of insolvent companies, reveal a marked variation between the frequency with which different routes are followed. Liquidations and receiverships are by far the most frequent with the options of administration and voluntary arrangement pursued by only a handful of all insolvent firms.

Table 1

Company Insolvencies in England and Wales

	1990	1991	1992	1993
Compulsory liquidations	5,997	8,368	9,732	8,361
Creditors' voluntary liquidations	9,074	13,459	14,692	12,464

Other Insolvency proceedings in England and Wales

	1990	1991	1992	1993
Administrative receiverships	4,318	7,515	8,312	5,362
Administrations	211	206	120	112
Voluntary arrangements	58	137	76	134
Other	1,884	4,587	7,858	2,962

Source: The Insolvency Service

Note: members' voluntary liquidations are not included becuse they are not associated with insolvency.

The Role of the Accountant
Accountants are involved in virtually every facet of the process of company insolvency, either as auditors, investigators, advisors or, most importantly,

insolvency practitioners.[1] From the time a firm senses that it is in trouble to the time its last assets are sold off, it will probably be dependent upon the actions of accountants. Moreover, accountants, when they serve as insolvency practitioners, generally have unlimited power over all aspects of a business, its assets and its staff. The following example, taken directly from the experiences of one unfortunate firm, should provide an adequate illustration of how important the role of the accountant can be.

In 1990, a long-established firm requested a second loan from its bank. The bank, sensing that the security of its first loan might be in trouble, called a major accountancy firm and requested that they send out an investigating auditor to ascertain the company's solvency. The accountant spent three days looking into the company's books, after which time he declared that the firm was de facto insolvent. On the basis of the investigating auditor's report, the bank decided to appoint administrators. To add insult to injury, the investigating accountant sent his bill to the unfortunate firm, not the bank that had requested the report.

The company launched a feverish protest, asserting that it was not only financially viable, but was actually earning a profit. The firm's assertion of financial viability was confirmed by an academic consultant who was in the process of advising the firm in its efforts to expand abroad.

The bank, on the basis of the investigating accountant's report, appointed administrators, astoundingly, from the very same firm of accountants. The administrators disagreed with the firm's view and concurred with the investigating accountant that the best hope for salvaging the bank's security was by dismantling the firm. The administrators set to work quickly, breaking up the firm up and selling off what it could.

The company, by now resigned to its fate, nevertheless protested that the administrators were selling off the company's assets at below the price they could fetch on the market. Subsequent events were to lend support to this assertion.

After the administrators had broken up and sold the "valuable" parts of the company, liquidators were called in to dispose of the remainder. Unbelievably, the liquidators, like the administrators and the investigative accountant, were from the same accountancy firm. Throughout the entire process of the dismemberment of the company, this one firm of accountants was collecting in excess of half a million pounds in fees, and the money for

[1] Insolvency Practitioners come from both the accountancy and legal professions. However, the majority of practitioners come from the accountancy profession.

these substantial fees was coming out of the coffers and assets of an "insolvent" company.

One final note is worth mentioning. The Managing Director of the company is now on income support. The firm of accountants is trying to get him declared personally bankrupt so that any income he earns over the next few years can be confiscated to pay creditors.

The Professional and Ethical Obligations of the Insolvency Practitioner
The accountant undoubtably plays a primary role in the operation of the insolvency system. Nevertheless, no uniform policy mechanism currently exists to regulate the conduct of accountants and insolvency practitioners in their dealings with troubled and insolvent firms. Rather, professional and ethical guidelines issued by the various accounting associations[1] are designed to ensure that accountants retain the public confidence. According to these guidelines, accountants and insolvency practitioners are generally expected, among other things, to:

1. maintain professional independence through integrity and an objective approach to professional work and remain free of any interest which might detract from objectivity, including personal or financial involvement with the client;
2. avoid using information gained professionally for personal gain;
3. avoid undertaking any work in which a minimum level of competence is not met;
4. perform all duties in a courteous and considerate manner.

As the case cited above should indicate, ethical guidelines do not always work to achieve an efficient outcome. For an accountant faced with financial pressures of a competitive market, the temptation to be led into ethically sensitive situations may prove too strong to resist. According to the Institute of Business Ethics (IBE), "In an economy run on market principles, the freedom allowed by society to its producers of goods and services is

---

[1] There are currently eight accountancy associations, most of which issue their own professional and/or ethical guidelines. However, since 50% of all practising insolvency practitioners are regulated by the Institute of Chartered Accountants, the ICAEW's "Guide to Professional Ethics" is currently the most relevant. The bulk of the remaining insolvency practitioners are regulated by the Insolvency Practitioner's Association and its "Guide to Professional Conduct and Ethics" (1987). The guidelines and standards of other professional bodies such as The Chartered Association of Certified Accountants, The Chartered Institute of Public Finance and Accounting, and The Chartered Institute of Management Accountants may occasionally come into play with the activities of an investigating accountant.

dependent on the degree to which the public has confidence in the integrity of its participants: the poorer the standard, the more regulations are needed" (Webley 1988 p1).

The problem facing the accountancy profession today is that it finds itself in a vigorously competitive market, and consequently the ethical guidelines and enforcement procedures which have sustained the profession for so long may no longer be adequate.

Professional Independence and Objectivity
Statement 20 of the Institute of Chartered Accountants of England and Wales' "Guide to Professional Ethics" sets out the specific guidelines for insolvency practitioners. The Statement declares that the "overriding importance in the [insolvency practitioner's] professional life is integrity and objectivity." Through integrity and objectivity, insolvency practitioners are supposed to maintain their professional independence. This is a state in which one is not influenced by any interests, personal, professional or financial, which might detract from his or her objectivity.

Conflicts of interest may impinge upon professional independence and objectivity anywhere there is a conflict between personal interest and the interest of the firm or its clients. All guidelines caution practitioners to avoid situations wherein a conflict of interest may arise. Nevertheless, the nature of possible conflicts are not well spelled out, leaving the individual practitioner or firm to determine when a conflict might or might not arise.

For instance, the guidelines declare that the practitioner should not accept appointments as a liquidator, supervisor of a voluntary arrangement, administrator, or receiver where there is a continuing professional relationship with a company. A "continuing professional relationship" (sometimes called a "material relationship") is where the practitioner is carrying out, or has carried out professional work for that client over the last three years. The guidelines then go on to say that this stricture does not apply where the appointment springs from the appointment by a creditor or interested party, unless the insolvency practitioner has previously been involved in the management of that particular company. This means that the practitioner, when appointed by a creditor or interested party, is allowed full freedom to act regardless of any prior professional relationship he or she may have with the company. The practitioner is assumed by the guidelines to possess the innate professional integrity to do what is right.

The guidelines do not, however, attempt to address the personal financial conflict of interest that may be inherent in a particular appointment. Thus, the practitioners mentioned in the case above were arguably acting with the full sanction of the ICA. Statement 20, section 24 of the ICA's guidelines declares:

> A practice or a principal in a practice may be appointed by a company to carry out an investigation at the instigation of a creditor or other party having an actual or potential financial interest in it, and the subsequent appointment of a principal in the practice as liquidator, administrator or administrative receiver of the company is not necessarily thereby rendered unacceptable.

Thus, in spite of the fact that the investigating accountant has a vested financial interest in declaring a company insolvent and garnering the subsequent fees for insolvency work, the woolly language of section 24 declares that the public need not worry about a conflict of interest arising. Admittedly, section 25 tries to interject some ethics by declaring that "such an appointment should not prevent the open discussion of the financial affairs of the company with the directors . . (or other)", but gives no indication of how such an "open discussion" is expected to occur.

The potential conflict of interest in having the investigating accountants, administrative receiver and liquidator all milking the same cow has not gone unnoticed by parties concerned with the future viability of firms. Two large accountancy firms, Kingston Smith and Rees Pollock, have declared that there can be a conflict of interest between the interests of a bank or a secured creditor and other creditors or management (Jack 18 June 1994). The British Chambers of Commerce has concurred (Jack 16 June 1994). Furthermore, even the ICAEW has added fuel to the critic's fire by admitting that 30 per cent of its members in a recent survey indicated that they thought that a conflict did arise when a banker appointed receivers from the same firm of accountants which conducted the investigation of the troubled firm (Jack 23 June 1994).

Perhaps the strongest evidence that commercial pressures may undermine an accountant's objectivity and give rise to a conflict of interest is revealed in the Royal Bank of Scotland's recent decision to employ different firms to act as investigators and receivers. Since instituting this policy, the rate of receiverships requested by the Bank has dropped by 60% (BBC Radio 4, "Face the Facts," 21 June 1994). This indicates that, if this drop is actually attributable to the unbundling of roles, then perhaps far too many firms are being forced into receivership and liquidation than is commercially necessary.

The Royal Bank of Scotland's experience provides evidence that there may well be an incipient conflict of interest whenever a firm or an individual serves as both investigating accountant and receiver. Accountancy firms may be no more immune to commercial pressure than the businesses that are subjected to a daily barrage of statutory regulation. The pressure to garner more and more fees, particularly if the accountant is a young associate hoping one day to be a partner in a big firm, can be intense. Nevertheless, there is currently nothing in the law, or even in the various professional guidelines, which prohibits an accountancy firm from wearing multiple, and often conflicting, hats in the system of insolvency.

The overwhelming majority of insolvency practitioners believe that there is nothing wrong with the current practice. The ICAEW, in spite of the dissention of 30 per cent of its members, believes that the conflict is "perceived rather than actual" (Jack 23 June 1994). Moreover, it maintains that the current system is cost-effective and efficient. Woolf (1994) of Levy Gee explains that "[a] bank will not appoint a receiver if there is any viable alternative and any insolvency practitioner who recommends this course, simply to improve his fees, will soon see his work dry up" (Woolf 21 June 1994). However, he continues, "Where a receivership is unavoidable, it is clearly cheaper and more efficient to have the same firm conduct the viability assessment and the receivership."

Some accountants have taken the suggestion of an actual conflict as a personal affront to their integrity. Mr Alan Griffiths of Grant Thornton declares: "It is a bit hard to stomach people doubting my professional integrity. I get my enjoyment from saving companies, not closing them down" (Jack 24 June 1994).

Ian Bond of Coopers and Lybrand maintains that "[t]hose . . . . . . who claim that the objectivity of the investigating accountant must appear to be unduly affected by the carrot of a subsequent administrative receivership are ignoring the basic facts about professional relationships" (Bond Insolvency Practitioner 1993 p31).

However, the "basic facts of professional relationships" are very far from clear today. In fact, many accountancy firms are discussing the possibility of abandoning the partnership form for a limited-liability partnership or even a company form (Economist 9 July 1994 73). The reasons for this potential sea-change in approach stem from the pressures of a radically different commercial and legal environment. Firms are bigger, more complex and more competitive than ever before. They face competition and threats of lawsuits from many quarters. In summary, the "professional relationship" relied on for so long by accountants and practitioners alike, increasingly does not exist.

The guidelines, therefore, may have a fundamental flaw in their operating premises; independence in appearance is often just as important as independence in fact. Few who read the bald facts presented in the illustration above could state unequivocally that independence was preserved.

Competence, Courtesy and Consideration

The issue of competence touches on not only the skill of the practitioner in the field of accountancy, but also on the individual's ability to utilise that skill in the particular context to which it is being applied. Yet accountants, particularly those acting as investigating accountants and as insolvency practitioners, have often been criticised as not understanding the operation of the businesses which they are entrusted to evaluate.

Accountants typically have no formal training or experience in the actual day-to-day operation of business. Rather, accountants spend most of their working lives looking at a business from a rule-oriented periphery. Unfortunately, when an accountant takes on the role of an insolvency practitioner, this lack of training and experience can mean that the accountant is not competent to undertake the creative task of rescuing a troubled, but viable, business. Nevertheless, the current insolvency system, which almost uniformly dispenses with experienced directors, generally leaves the insolvency practitioner in complete and total charge of the firm and its assets. Thus, the accountant's ethical obligation to avoid undertaking work in which a minimum level of competence is not met, would appear, in light of the aims and objectives of the law, not to be fulfilled at least from the perspective of troubled businesses. The last stated objective of the law, as mentioned above, was that insolvency practitioners should seek, where possible, to facilitate the rescue of companies. For technically-minded accountants, however, the straightforward route to liquidation may be much more obvious than the tortuous route to recovery.

A related criticism, which can be addressed to the entire UK insolvency system, is that it is biased toward "ruination" (Gladstone and Lee 1994). Put another way, Britain does not have a "rescue culture," the absence of which necessarily colours the approach of practitioners (Goldstein 1993). According to the Institute of Chartered Accountants "Guide to Professional Ethics", accountants are obliged to be courteous and considerate in the performance their duties. The question arises as to why the obligation to be courteous and considerate needed to be included in the guidelines at all if the integrity and good will of accountants are per se beyond reproach. Investigative accountants and insolvency practitioners have quite frequently been chastened for their poor "bedside manner". In spite of the obligation to be polite, the fact remains that the prime responsibility of an investigating accountant is to the debenture holder who initiated his appointment (*Insolvency Practitioner* 1993 p31) and the prime responsibility of the practitioner is to the creditors.

Further support for the view that the system is biased toward "ruination" is to be found in the neglect of the CVA procedure which was expressly introduced with a view toward meeting the last stated objective, that of facilitating the rehabilitation of companies. However, as discussed above, the CVA procedure has received little attention from practitioners. Practitioners argue that they do not employ the CVA procedure because it is inherently flawed. First, they maintain, the procedure can take years to set up and complete, making it difficult for the firm to obtain continuing credit. There is also no statutory stay allowed for the contemplation of the procedure, so that once it becomes obvious that a CVA is being considered, creditors claims often come flooding in, thereby eliminating the possibility of setting the CVA up (*Insolvency Bulletin* 1992 p7).

However, at least one well-known practitioner disagrees with his colleagues claimed defences (Goldstein 1993). Goldstein believes that the CVA procedure is not only viable, but highly effective. He sees it as a way of helping a company work its way out of trouble, thereby preserving assets while simultaneously paying creditors. He complains that practitioners are far too reliant on the liquidation route which is easier to undertake and more remunerative in the short term.

In 1993, the popularity of the CVA procedure grew somewhat, with 134 arrangements being structured, as opposed to 76 in 1992. Some of this increase can be credited to the public relations efforts of the DTI, but the main reason seems to be the end of the recession which has given creditors more confidence in firms' future prospects. This increase, though nearly 100 per cent, nevertheless represents a tiny percentage of over 20,000 total insolvencies. Whether a proposed simplification of the CVA procedure leads to a further increase in its usage in 1995 remains to be seen. The Law Society has recently endorsed the suggestion that a moratorium be placed on creditors' rights prior to a creditors meeting, a recommendation that will greatly increase the procedures attractiveness to troubled firms, but which is violently opposed by banks and most insolvency practitioners.

In conclusion, the issue may either be one of the accountant's competence to understand the merits of the CVA route or it may be a question of the accountant's integrity in selecting the easier and more familiar routes. Whatever the conclusion, the problem of the incompatibility of the accountant's approach and the needs of an ailing business will remain a dilemma as long as the current system of insolvency remains in operation.

The Profession's Efforts at Reform

Accountancy firms, besides being professional bodies, are also firms with assets and debts, profits and losses. As such, they must balance delicately the interests of the firm and its balance sheet and the interests of the public it exists to serve.

In the field of insolvency, the profession is not seen by many as achieving the correct balance. According to Chris Hughes of Cork Gully, "the existing law in too many cases still amounts to a prescription to bayonet the wounded" (Jack 1993). Perhaps the pressures to make money are too great and the public interest too remote or perhaps the ethical guidelines are too weak. It would appear, however, that as the standard exhibited by investigating accountants and insolvency practitioners is increasingly under the influence of the same market pressures as many businesses, that regulation of the insolvency practitioners profession may be needed to ensure that "the public retains confidence in the integrity of its participants".

The insolvency profession has not entirely ignored the growing criticism of its conduct. It recently launched its own self-regulating body, the Joint Insolvency Monitoring Unit (JIMU or the "Unit") after sustained pressure from the Insolvency Service and the DTI. This unit composed of three chartered accountancy institutes, a selection of certified accountants, the DTI and the Institute of Practitioners of Insolvency. Its remit is to inspect all insolvency practitioners every three to five years to ensure that they are abiding by their statutory obligations. Reports of the inspections are submitted to the ICAEW and the Insolvency Practitioners' Association who then determine if any disciplinary actions are necessary. Recently, insolvency practitioners have criticised the aggressive style of the new Unit. The Unit mandates the completion of a pre-inspection questionnaire which some practitioners view as potentially self-incriminating. The Insolvency Practitioners' Association complained that they had expected the Unit to help its members comply with regulation and not to discipline them (Jack 21 June 1994).

Thus, the Unit will not ensure that insolvency practitioners follow the letter and the spirit of the guidelines to which they ascribe. Rather, the various professional bodies will still be responsible for disciplining their members. Nor will the Unit ensure that insolvency practitioners have a working knowledge of business so that they understand the operations of the company whose fate they hold in their hands. Meeting these two criteria is, unfortunately, still up to the individual and his or her conscience.

Future Suggestions for Reform

Creating a suitable mix of ethical guidelines and regulations will require a lot of work as well as a sea-change in the philosophy of the profession and therefore will not be easy. Nevertheless, certain minimum changes appear to be necessary if the system of insolvency is ever to fulfil the role for which it was intended.

First, the unlimited authority of the insolvency practitioner over the assets of the failed or troubled firm must be broken. Second, accountants and insolvency practitioners must be made publicly accountable. That is, they must be made to answer for their actions before the law, not solely before their peers in the profession. Third, accountants and insolvency practitioners must be made to owe a duty of care to the failed firm as well as to the appointing firm. Fourth, insolvency procedures should be structured to encourage creditors and shareholders to put a firm's assets toward their most productive uses (Aghion et al). The entire insolvency system must be imbued with the desire to rescue viable firms.

References

Aghion, Philippe, Oliver Hart and John Moore "A Proposal for Bankruptcy Reform in the U.K." *Insolvency Law & Practice* Vol 9 No 4 1993 pp 103–108.
Benzie, A.G. (1986) "Changes to Liquidation Procedures" in *Insolvency: Companies, Directors and the New Legislation* Guildford College of Law Lectures
Berry, Christopher and Steve Hill (1989) "Bankruptcy: Avoiding the Loss of the Matrimonial Home" *The Law Society's Gazette* (12 April) pp 14–19
Bolton Committee (1971) *Small Firms: Report of the Committee of Inquiry on Small Firms* Cmnd 4811 Her Majesty's Stationery Office London
Coopers and Lybrand (1992) *Solutions for Business* London
Cork, Sir Kenneth (1980) *Bankruptcy: Interim Report of the Insolvency Law Review Committee* London Her Majesty's Stationery Office
Cork Gully (1991) *Annual Review 1991* Cork Gully London
Cork Gully (1991) *Insolvency in Brief* Cork Gully London
Cottell, Philip G. Jr., and Terry M. Perlin (1990) *Accounting Ethics: A Practical Guide for Professionals* London Quorum Books

County NatWest WoodMac (1991) "Company Pathology" *Equity Briefing Paper* CNWM(7) London

Cressy, Robert C. (1992) "Small Firm Debt Rescheduling versus Insolvency: The Bank's Decision Problem" *Warwick Business School SME Centre Working Paper Series No 9*

Curran, James and Robert A. Blackburn (1992) "Small Firms and Local Economic Networks: Relations Between Small Large Firms in Two Localities" *Kingston Business School Business Paper Series*

The Economist (1992) "When Firms Go Bust" 1 September pp 67–71

Gladstone, Bryan (1993) *Rescue or Ruination: A Comparison of Approaches to Small Business Insolvency and Bankruptcy between the United States and the United Kingdom* MSc. in Entrepreneurial Studies Scottish Enterprise Foundation University of Stirling

Gladstone, Bryan and Jennifer Lee (1994) *The Operation of the Insolvency System in the U.K.: Some Implications for Entrepreneurialism* Small Business Economics, February 1994

Goldstein, Mark (1993) *Treasury Management,* forthcoming

Goode, R. M. (1990) *Principles of Corporate Insolvency Law* London, Sweet and Maxwell

Griffiths, Michael and Stuart Williams (1986) *The 1986 Insolvency and Companies Legislation* CAET London

Hobson, Rodney (1990) "Creditors Recover More with Voluntary Schemes" *The Times* 13 January

Hoppitt, Julian (1987) *Risk and Failure in English Business 1700–1800* Cambridge, Cambridge University Press

Insolvency Bulletin (1992) "CVA Who is Doing It?" November 7

Jack, Andrew (1993) "Insolvency Law Seen as Bayoneting the Wounded" *Financial Times* January 21 p 8

Jack, Andrew (1994) "Chambers Attack Insolvency Laws" *Financial Times* March 2

Jack, Andrew (1994) "Complaints Against Accountants Rise 8%" *Financial Times* June 7

Jack, Andrew (1994) "Debate Reopens on Accountant's Insolvency Role" *Financial Times* June 7

Jack, Andrew (1994) "Firm's Warn on Conflict of Interest: Fears Over Role of Investigating Accountants Grow in Receivership Debate" *Financial Times* June 18

Jack, Andrew (1994) "Insolvency Firms Attack 'Aggressive' Watchdog" *Financial Times* June 21

Jack, Andrew (1994) "Society Defends Insolvency Practice" *Financial Times* June 23

Jack, Andrew (1994), "For What We Are About to Receive: Andrew Jack on Tensions Over the Role of Investigative Accountants" *Financial Times* June 24

Jones, Beverly (1993) "Insolvency and the balance sheet" *Insolvency Law and Practice* Vol 9(5) pp133–136

Krasner, Gerald (1992), "Corporate Voluntary Arrangements" *Insolvency Bulletin* November 8–10

London Business School (1987) *A Study to Determine the Reasons for Failure of Small Businesses in the UK* London, Stoy Hayward and NatWest Bank

McQueen, John (1992) *Bankruptcy: The Reality and the Law*, Lancaster: The Bankruptcy Association of Great Britain and Ireland

Morriss, Christopher (1994) "Cross-border rescues and asset recovery – problems and solutions" *Insolvency Law and Practice* Vol 10(2) pp42–46

Ratford, W.F. et al (1985) *A Guide to the Insolvency Act 1985* London Financial Training Publications Ltd

Sealy, Michael and David Milman (1988) *Annotated Guide to the 1986 Insolvency Legislation* London CCH Editions

Stein, R. (1993) "You Can't Blame It All on Banks" *Today* 26 February 34

Storey, D.J. Keasey, K. Watson, R. and Wynarczyk (1987) *The Performance of Small Firms, Profits, Jobs and Failures* London Croom Helm

Webly, Simon (1988) "Company Philosophies and Codes of Business Ethics" London The Institute of Business Ethics

Woolf, Derrick S. "Letters to the Editor: No Conflict in Investigating Accountant's Becoming Receivers" June 21

Wren, Colin (1987) "Closure Rates among Assisted and Non-Assisted Establishments" *Regional Studies* 22(2) pp107–119

Index